PRAISE FOR:

Wrapped in Grace:
Finding Power in Praise and Peace in His Presence

How grateful I am for a book that enables me to share the words from Beth's heart, who truly has a heart for God. I've read daily devotionals for years, but the words that Beth writes linger with me through the day and assure His love for all. Her words reveal the joy and awesomeness of a personal relationship with our Heavenly Father, demonstrating the relationship she has and the one He desires with everyone.

In a world that challenges us and changes daily, His love never changes. He is constantly by our side, just waiting for us to acknowledge that we need Him, and He is there—always revealing Himself and always providing what we need. Beth's devotions are trustworthy and warm the heart. They are memorable, thoughtful, and enlightening. They are what devotionals should be, pointing us directly to God and sharing His words. I am excited that her book will allow me to share what she so graciously shares.

—**Linda Bingham Hensley, Author and Illustrator of *The Little Turtle Book Series* for children.**

Wrapped in Grace is a timely and soul-refreshing work that gently leads readers into the steady, sustaining presence of God. Beth Mims writes with a rare blend of tenderness and truth, reminding us that grace is not merely a theological concept, but the very strength that carries us through life's joys, sorrows, and uncertainties.

As an ordained minister and a retired Army Chief Warrant Officer 4, I understand the weight of endurance, discipline, and perseverance. This book speaks directly to those moments when faith must be lived, not just believed. Through lyrical prose and thoughtful reflection, *Wrapped in Grace* offers comfort to the weary, hope to those in prolonged trials, and peace to hearts seeking rest in God's presence.

Beth Mims has a gift for inviting readers into praise—even in difficult seasons—and for pointing them back to the truth that God's grace is sufficient in every circumstance. This is a book to be read slowly, prayed through deeply, and returned to often.

I wholeheartedly recommend *Wrapped in Grace* to anyone longing to experience the renewing power of God's grace in their daily walk.

— Anthony Hayes, Ordained Minister and Retired U.S. Army Chief Warrant Officer 4 (CW4)

Wrapped In Grace

Finding Power In Praise And Peace In His Presence

Beth Mims

All rights reserved. This book is protected by the copyright laws of the United States of America. This book may not be copied or reprinted for commercial gain or profit. The use of short quotations or occasional page copying for personal or group study is permitted and encouraged.

Unless otherwise noted, Scripture quotations used in this book are from *The Holy Bible*, King James Version. © 1973, 1978, 1984, 2011 International Bible Society. Used by permission of Zondervan Bible Publishers.

Copyright © 2026 Beth Mims. All rights reserved.

Wrapped in Grace: Finding Power In Praise And Peace In His Presence, Beth Mims
Issued in electronic and paperback formats
Paperback ISBN: 978-1-970354-05-8
E-book ISBN: 978-1-970354-06-5
LCCN: 2026901367
First Edition

Publisher: Dressed in Love Press, LLC
www.drkatherinehayes.com

Cover Designer: Katherine Hutchinson-Hayes
Book Interior Designer: Jenifer Jennings

Printed in the United States of America

To Eddy, Leslie and Jenna, my best teachers and constant inspirations and always for the glory of God.

Table of Contents

Foreword 1
Wrapped in Grace 3
Grace for the Rootbound 4
Fighting Battles with the Grace of God 7
What Does Wisdom Look Like? 10
Grace to Battle the Darkness 13
When Darkness Seems to Win 15
The Grace to Dig Out Stumps 16
Finding Grace to Deal with Ants 19
Me: A Showcase of His Grace 21
Grace for Everyday Obedience 23
Grace for the Martha Souls 26
Unable: And Then There Was Grace 29
Grace for Eating Issues: Reading Your Bible 31
Grace to Pray Like David 35
Grace When Passing Through 38
Today 40
Dare to Be a Daniel 41
Five Principles of Praise 44
Grace Under the Refrigerator 47
Grace Gives Us Glad Songs 49
Five Smooth Stones for Today 51
Grace to Remember 53
Grace to Cast Your Care on God 56
Grace to Follow Hard After God 58
Grace for Hard Lessons 60
Vitamins for the Soul 63
Grace for the Struggle 66
God Is 69
Grace Isn't Stagnant 70

Grace When Malware Strikes 73
What's in a Name? 76
Trophy of Grace 79
Grace to Be a Barnabas 80
Grace When We Are Wilting 83
Send Down the Rain 86
Grace for Everyday Cleaning 87
Send Down the Hail 90
Grace to do the Right Things 93
Passion 96
I Want to Love Him So Much 98
Words of Grace 99
Shine On 101
Grace to Rejoice Always 102
Always With Me 105
Grace to Make the Best Choices 107
God in His Grace Provides 110
Grace When I am Tossed About 112
Running on My Knees 115
Intercessors 117
Grace to Deal with Questions 118
Grace in Every Circumstance 121
Seasons of Grace 124
Reviving Hope: Grace Lessons From Resilient Ferns 125
Grace to Live by Faith in All Life's Seasons 127
Grace During Seasons of Stress 131
Keeper of My Heart 135
Grace that Gives Joy in All Seasons of Life 136
Grace in Seasons of Crisis 139
Grace that Lives in Gratitude 142
Grace in Seasons of Anxiety 145
Grace for Seasons of Waiting 148

Grace for Impossible Seasons 151
Grace to Continue 154
Place of Grace 157
Grace for the Pruning Season 158
Grace for Seasons of Learning 161
Grace is My Credential for All Seasons 164
Saving Grace 167
Grace for the Lost 168
Rescued 171
Grace in Failure 172
Grace When the Storm Comes: Situational Awareness 175
God's Unchanging Grace 179
Grace for Wise Building 182
Bad News and Then There's Grace 185
Grace for the Broken 188
Grace for a Letter from Paul 191
Grace for the End Times 194
Secure 197
God's Magnum Opus: His Grace Magnified 198
Resources 201
6-Week Study Guide for Reflection, Prayer, and Growth 202
Leader's Guide & 6-Week Study 206
Prayer & Reflection Page 209
Acknowledgements 210

Foreword

Grace, the unmerited favor of God, is a word that Christians sprinkle in conversations. We depend on it for salvation, but we often take it for granted. We sing about it, but we fail to see how intricately it weaves in and out of our daily lives.

Wrapped up in God's boundless love, grace stands as the most powerful condition for happiness and life. It breeds hope and second chances. Grace lives through Jesus Christ as our connection to God and eternal life.

Just as grace connects us to God, it connects us to other people. Think of the varying forms of the word—gracious, graciousness, graciously. Grace is the softness of life, the refreshing rain that washes and cleanses. It buffs the rough edges and charms the wild. There is no aspect of life that cannot be touched and bettered by grace.

Grace carries forgiveness.

Grace lives in gratitude.

Grace grants pardon, approval, and favor.

Grace gives strength to take the next step, carry the burden, love one more time.

Grace stands in the face of hatred and hurt, and grace survives.

Grace is a gift that has its beginning and ending in God. We cannot earn it, so God offers it freely through His Son.

We talk about the grace given to us through Christ's death on the cross, the grace that saves us through faith. We don't deserve this grace, which offers forgiveness and redemption from sin and death. It is a gift, paid for by Christ's sacrifice. We access this grace simply by trusting Him.

We talk about the grace to get through the difficult situations we face in this world, strength for each day, joy in trials, and provision in hard times. We know that this grace comes from the hand of God.

There is no other explanation. We depend on His grace daily to maneuver through the messes in this world, and He is faithful to supply our needs as we look to Him and daily trust Him. It is this grace that provides laughter when the coffee spills and the children's homework gets ruined. It is this grace that enables us to hug the offender when our hearts are broken.

And then there are the seasons of grace. The seasons that seem to stretch over eons, through illness and extended trial. Times when we go day to day, unsure of next steps and next breaths. Times when God seems silent and we must wait, and waiting is so hard. During these seasons, we live by faith, we walk by faith, and we depend on God's grace, even when we don't realize it, to see us through. These seasons stretch over weeks, months, or even years as we lean into the faithfulness of God, wrapped in His wondrous grace.

God's grace permeates every moment of every day of our lives, and He is always revealing Himself to us through His word and through His world and through His people. We only need open hearts and eyes to see Him and ears to hear Him.

If you are a believer, I hope you see yourself wrapped in His grace as you read these pages. If you do not know Christ, I pray that these pages will make you thirsty for Him. He longs to wrap you in His grace and hold you close to His heart.

"Therefore being justified by faith, we have peace with God through our Lord Jesus Christ: By whom also we have access by faith into this grace wherein we stand, and rejoice in hope of the glory of God" (Romans 5:1–2, KJV).

Wrapped in Grace

Just a tot
She stands as a queen,
Blanket wrapped around
like a regal train.
Her security.
Guarded from the terrors
of this world
by its very presence.
She breathes in deeply
as she faces the world's tempests
She holds it tight
and marches forward.

No blanket,
I stand here chosen,
wrapped in grace that flows
to cover my soul.
My security.
Guarded from the terrors
of this life
by His very presence.
I breathe out prayer
as I face the world's tempests
He holds me tight,
and I march forward.

Grace for the Rootbound

But grow in grace, and in the knowledge of our Lord and Saviour Jesus Christ. To him be glory both now and for ever. Amen.
—2 Peter 3:18, KJV

"God cares more about our character than about our comfort."
—Rick Warren, *The Purpose Driven Life*[1]

I have been repotting plants that are long overdue for new homes, so the term rootbound is heavy on my mind (and back).

Plants become rootbound when left in one pot for too long. The roots continue to grow, and gradually the nutrients are depleted, leaving little soil for the plant. The plant may look healthy and even continue to bloom for a while, but it really needs attention.

You can tell if a plant is rootbound when you try to remove it from the pot, and it retains the pot's shape. Rootbound plants are not unusual; in fact, many plants that you purchase from a store are rootbound when you bring them home. That is one reason it is important to transplant them soon after purchase.

If you remove a rootbound plant from its pot and just slap it into a larger pot, the roots will keep growing in the same tangled directions. This means that the plant may not fully utilize the soil in which it is placed. Haphazard gardener that I am, I have pulled up plants whose entire root balls looked exactly the same as when I transplanted them from their store pots to my containers.

And then I wonder why it did not flourish.

Dealing with a rootbound plant is not pretty. In fact, it requires a certain amount of bravery to take a lovely flower and pull its roots apart before planting. Sometimes the gardener must use a knife to cut the roots so that they can be spread out, and scissors can come in handy to cut off the lengthy roots at the bottom. The reward, however, is a healthier plant that can flourish and sustain through the changing seasons.

I am not qualified to give gardening advice here; I was kind when I called myself a haphazard gardener. I have been thinking about this a lot, though, and I find some similarities to my own life.

There have been times in my life when I settled into a routine that became so comfortable that I no longer had to stretch to complete my duties each day. I was planning my work and working my plan, content to rise, work, worship, sleep, and repeat day after day. My community of others was small and controlled, and I was satisfied.

But I was not growing. I was rootbound.

Others may or may not have noticed. To be honest, I didn't notice either until the Master Gardener decided to repot me with new responsibilities, a new community, and a new schedule. The repotting process was not something I sought, and it was not comfortable.

Just as I had to beat on some of my pots to dislodge the rootbound plants, and just as I had to cut apart some of the root systems, God used trial, challenge, and discipline to shock me out of my routine and focus my eyes on Him alone. It was a jolt.

I have ferns that I have repotted numerous times. Each time I attack them, I end up with multiple plants from each existing plant. I spread their roots out in new soil, fertilize and water them, and watch them grow. They usually look scraggly the first few weeks, but then they take off. I notice new shoots and a greener color, and the new pots begin to fill with growth. It is amazing.

When I think of God's repotting process, I think of the numerous examples He gives us in scripture. Think about how God worked in Joseph's life, in Abraham's, in Daniel's, and we could go on to mention Moses, Paul, Peter, Matthew, and so many others. God is in the growing business, even when it means repotting rootbound people.

God has had to repot me several times in my life. Each time stretched me, and each time I lost some old roots that were hampering growth in my life—things like resignation, self-sufficiency, self-dependence, apathy in my comfort zone, and pride. Each time He provided soil to support new growth—things like an expanded community of believers, fresh eyes for His word, more focused prayer, and new challenges in ministry. Sometimes, my new pot required a physical move, and every time it required movement in my heart.

I don't have to be rootbound. If I'm living in God's plan, the place or places of planting will sustain growth. I don't want to stagnate and fail to grow and bloom because I am so comfortable in my pot that I don't want to move. God doesn't want that for me either. He will keep me growing if I stay in His word and connected to Him through prayer and fellowship.

But He is not afraid to repot me if I allow myself to become complacently rootbound either.

Healthy plants grow and produce blooms. Healthy Christians do, too.

Father, help me not to become complacent and rootbound where You have planted me. Keep me growing, active, and blooming for You. Help me to grow in Your word and in fellowship with You and with Your children. Use me in Your work, Lord. Thank You for all you do in my life.

Think About It:
- Are there times when you become rootbound (stuck in place) in your life and service for God?
- How does God deal with you?
- What can you do when you are feeling rootbound?

Fighting Battles with the Grace of God

For though we walk in the flesh, we do not war after the flesh: (For the weapons of our warfare are not carnal, but mighty through God to the pulling down of strong holds;) Casting down imaginations, and every high thing that exalteth itself against the knowledge of God, and bringing into captivity every thought to the obedience of Christ;
—2 Corinthians 10:3–5

I don't like to think about having enemies, but I have them. Sometimes, they are my thoughts that race like runaway trains through my brain. Other times, they involve conflicts that I didn't ask for with people in my sphere of influence, misunderstandings that I can't seem to find any way around. Jesus talked in John chapter fifteen about his followers being hated by the world, and sometimes, no matter how hard I try, these conflicts happen.

David, the shepherd boy who became king, the man after God's own heart, faced enemies.

He confronted Goliath, the giant, and the victory was swift and decisive.

He faced the lion in the field, and the lion proved to be no match against his skill.

His battle with Saul, the king who preceded him, was different, though. That battle was not one David sought, but it stretched for years over mountains and across desert land. He hid in caves and faced great hardship. Finally, the battle ended with Saul's death. The conflict was confusing, frustrating, and guilt-ridden for David. He didn't want to fight Saul, but survival forced his hand.

David was a mighty warrior, so a direct attack with a clear mission caused him little angst. The cat-and-mouse game that Saul forced him into, however, sapped him emotionally and spiritually. This battle brought with it skirmishes with the enemies of fear and doubt (Psalm 35:22), feelings of being forsaken (Psalm 22), and guilt (Psalm 38) over his conduct and his conflict with the king. Read through his prayers and petitions in the book of Psalms to see where, over and over again, he cried out to God.

There is good news about David, though. No matter what conflict he was facing, he cried out to God. He may have been flinging questions and challenges, but he was aiming them in the right direction.

With God's help, David had downed Goliath with one smooth river stone. He faced the enemies of his soul, however, with praise and petition, confession and repentance, and an overwhelming trust in his Sustainer and Redeemer, the God Who saves.

Today, I am much more apt to struggle with uncertainties and confusion than I am to face a giant or a lion. Still, those enemies of the soul, the nagging doubts and fears that tear at faith, the spiraling thoughts that disrupt peace and sleep, the sins that seem to overtake again and again are troublesome and spiritually debilitating.

Paul reminds me in 2 Corinthians 3:4 that my weapons for these battles (and they are battles) are not carnal (of the flesh), but mighty through God. Just as God gave David victory over Goliath, He has provided the weapons I need for the warfare with my flesh.

Like David, I want to face life's daily skirmishes that my fleshly enemies present with weapons given to me by God. So, when the opponents come knocking, I will respond with praise to God, with constant petition to God, with confession of my need, with repentance of my failings, and with overwhelming trust in the God who is my Portion, my Sustainer, my Deliverer, my Salvation.

He alone holds the victory!

Heavenly Father, thank You for providing the weapons that I need to fight the battles that I face in this life. Strengthen me to respond to You with praise when my thoughts spiral out of control. Help me remember to turn every care over to You and confess every need to You. Let me run to You quickly when I fail, knowing Your arms of grace are waiting to wrap around me. I trust You, my portion, my sustainer, my deliverer, my salvation. You are my victory.

Think About It:
- What enemies are you facing today?
- How can you use God's weapons of praise, prayer, confession, repentance, and trust to battle against these enemies?

What Does Wisdom Look Like?

But the wisdom that is from above is first pure, then peaceable, gentle, and easy to be intreated, full of mercy and good fruits, without partiality, and without hypocrisy.
—James 3:17

Our world is in dire need of wisdom. We survive off fragments of information, distorted by the perspectives of those who spout them. Truth is treated as a variable, dependent on the situation, rather than an absolute to guide our thinking and our walk.

Knowledge is overflowing, but we struggle to know what to do with the avalanche of information that overwhelms us each day. We don't know how to apply what we know. The appropriate use of knowledge is guided by wisdom, but what does wisdom look like?

According to James 3:17, *wisdom is pure*—untainted by the whims of human flesh and the foibles of mankind. It comes from God, and it is characterized, at least partially, by what is missing from it—no envying or strife. In other words, wisdom is not about making me look good or getting my own way. It doesn't seek harm for others. Wisdom from God focuses on the good, the right, the righteous (Philippians 4:8).

Wisdom is peaceable. It doesn't look for an argument or an opening in the conversation into which it can insert itself. Wisdom allows time for thought and is not combative. It does not seek to prove a point, because it is the point.

Wisdom is gentle. The correction it brings is offered with love and seeks the best for the other. It works to encourage rather than tear down.

Wisdom is easy to be entreated or to reason with. It doesn't put up fences of self-preservation and defensiveness because it relies on truth. Given truth, wisdom sits up and pays attention.

Wisdom is full of mercy and good fruits. A person who operates in wisdom won't be found hiding in darkness. Instead, he will be open and generous, looking to serve.

Wisdom is without partiality. It serves everyone. There is no preferential treatment or one-upmanship with wisdom.

Wisdom is without hypocrisy. What you see is what you get—today, tomorrow, whenever. It works without pretense. Wisdom does not consider political correctness, or the "right," or the "left." Wisdom operates in truth, unfettered by the interpretation of current trends.

When you look at the characteristics of wisdom, they look a lot like the fruits of the Holy Spirit. "But the fruit of the Spirit is love, joy, peace, longsuffering, gentleness, goodness, faith, Meekness, temperance: against such there is no law" (Galatians 5:22).

That's because wisdom comes only from God. We can't learn it in a university or through an online course. It grows in our lives as we yield our will and our thoughts to the truth of the word of God and to the leadership of His Spirit.

The good news is that wisdom is free. Do you need wisdom?

"If any of you lack wisdom, let him ask of God, that giveth to all men liberally, and upbraideth not; and it shall be given him. But let him ask in faith, nothing wavering. For he that wavereth is like a wave of the sea driven with the wind and tossed" (James 1:5-6).

God wants us to have the wisdom we need to navigate the hard places of this life. We look for it in self-help books and talk shows. He says, "Ask Me. I will give it to you." The one condition that He gives is that we ask in faith. If we read the rest of the book of James, we find that faith results in works. In other words, when we ask in faith, we do so with the intention of acting on the wisdom God provides.

I think about that old commercial, "Got Milk?" when I read the first chapter of James. I look at my life and ask, "Got Wisdom?" James tells me what wisdom looks like, so that I can evaluate its characteristics in my life.[2]

Are you in need of wisdom in the situations you face today?

God has an unlimited supply. Just ask.

Father, I need wisdom to navigate this world each day. It is a maze that confuses and wearies me. Your word is the light for my path and the lamp for my feet. Help me to understand and apply what You teach me in Your word. Grant me wisdom to discern the right and wrong in this mixed-up society. Let my life reflect the characteristics of Your wisdom and not the false wisdom of this world. May I be faithful to speak Your truth always. In your precious Son's name I pray.

Think About It:

- What characteristics of wisdom are present or missing from your life?
- In what areas of your life do you need wisdom? Do you pray for God to give you wisdom?

Grace to Battle the Darkness

For God has not given us the spirit of fear, but of power, and of love, and of a sound mind.
—2 Timothy 1:7

Ask any child—terror lives in the darkness. Turn out the light, and the bogeyman comes out in full force, fueled by the unknown and the ever-active imagination.

One of the first verses I taught our children was Psalm 56:3: "What time I am afraid, I will trust in Thee."

We said it every night. We said it every night to combat fear with TRUTH.

Today, my children are grown, but the darkness still lives. Shadows of evil and destruction cover our world, and it is easy to allow terror to take over. And that is just what the enemy wants.

The enemy calls us to fear, but God calls us to faith.

There is only one way to combat the fear that the enemy is selling. We must fight fear with TRUTH. God is the Source of all TRUTH, and He has given us His word to teach us His TRUTH.

Thumb through Psalms and grasp just a few of the verses that replace fear with faith.

"The LORD is my rock, and my fortress, and my deliverer; my God, my strength, in whom I will trust; my buckler, and the horn of my salvation, and my high tower" (Psalm 18:2).

"Yea, though I walk through the valley of the shadow of death, I will fear no evil: for Thou art with me; Thy rod and Thy staff they comfort me" (Psalm 23:4).

"The LORD is my light and my salvation; whom shall I fear? the LORD is the strength of my life; of whom shall I be afraid?" (Psalm 27:1).

"Be of good courage, and He shall strengthen your heart, all ye that hope in the LORD" (Psalm 31:24).

"Thou art my hiding place; Thou shalt preserve me from trouble; Thou shalt compass me about with songs of deliverance" (Psalm 32:7).

You can keep thumbing; the TRUTH is there. God is bigger than our trouble. He is bigger than our fear. In the darkness of this world, He is our Light.

So, read His TRUTH and say His TRUTH every day.

Say it. Sing it. Shout it. Believe it, and let it live in your heart.

"Who hath delivered us from the power of darkness, and hath translated us into the kingdom of his dear Son" (Colossians 1:13).

Father, thank You for the truth of Your word. Thank You for giving light that is brighter than any darkness that I face. Thank You for delivering me from the power of Satan's darkness. Help me to live in Your light every day. In the powerful name of Jesus, I pray.

Think About It:
- When are you the most afraid?
- Do you use God's Word to help you when you are afraid? What verses help you the most?

When Darkness Seems to Win

Down through the eons darkness flies—
Carried by Adam's fatal fall.
Fueling the struggles that haunt mankind—
Trying to drown the Savior's call.

How deeply the darts of darkness pierce.
How bitter the wounds that scar the soul.
Is there a balm to heal the sores?
Is there a salve that can make us whole?

Suffering the brutal pains of death,
Christ bore our blackness as His own;
Briefly, the darkness seemed to win
when He hung defeated and alone.

But darkness cannot quench the Light
nor snuff the candle's flickering flare;
Death did not have the final say
on Messiah, bruised and bare.

He arose and conquered Satan's plan
Threw off the chains of darkest night,
Took back what Satan thought he had
And banished darkness with His light.

Sometimes the darkness seems to win
squelching the light of hurting souls
But always Christ's great Light breaks through,
Shattering darkness, making whole.

The Grace to Dig Out Stumps

Search me, O God, and know my heart: try me, and know my thoughts: And see if there be any wicked way in me, and lead me in the way everlasting.
—Psalm 139:23-24

Several years ago, we cut down an enormous tree in our side yard. The stump that was left was unsightly, and I didn't like it, so I took it upon myself to hire someone to grind it off. They did, and the grass grew over the scar in the ground. It looked good, and I was happy.

Several years passed, and I forgot all about that tree—and the stump.

Recently, when we decided to expand the parking space and driveway, that decision came back to haunt me.

My husband began to remove grass and dirt to level the ground in that area, and under the ground was the stump. (I know it was at least the size of the Rock of Gibraltar.) I had forgotten all about it, but there it was—in the way.

My suggestion was to pave over it. I believe in covering things up. My husband, though, knew it had to come out. If left, the stump would continue to rot and gradually cause the pavement to sink in that area.

For two days, he dug, and we pulled. He cut smaller roots from the stump and dug some more. I cheered him on and provided ice water, but I really wasn't much help. Gradually, though, he was able to dig deeply enough to get a chain around that stump and pull it out with the truck. It still had to be cut up and burned.

My husband was gracious, but he did remind me that the job would have been easier if the stump had been dealt with when it was ground down. In other words, my solution of just getting it out of sight was not enough.

As I watched him labor and sweat over that stump, I thought how easy it is to allow stumps to hide in my heart. I am hurt or I sin or there is this attitude that keeps cropping up, and instead of dealing with the issue, I just gloss over it and go on my merry way. Out of sight, out of mind.

Sooner or later, though, the stump shows up again. Sooner or later, something disturbs the surface, revealing the stump in my heart. I think I am in good shape, but then—the stump.

Heart stumps stump me more than I like to think, and just like that stump in the yard caused my husband hard, straining work, they can harm the people I love. They affect my attitude and my witness.

How much better to deal with the hurt or the disappointment or the sin immediately. How much better to take that stump to the cross and allow Jesus to dig it out. How much better to confess the stump immediately and access God's healing power.

I find myself checking for stumps these days. Are there any of them hiding that will one day show up to haunt me?

I need God's help—first, to identify the stumps (sins, attitudes, hurts, bitterness). Then I can confess them to Him. He is faithful to forgive and to help me get rid of them.

I am so thankful that God is in the stump-digging business. He is faithful and just to dig them out when I open my heart to Him.

"If we confess our sins, he is faithful and just to forgive us our sins, and to cleanse us from all unrighteousness" (1 John 1:9).

Father, search my heart today and see if there are hidden stumps of sin or wrong attitudes that are troubling my life or hindering my relationship with You. Help me to confess them to you so that you can cleanse me fully of anything that does not align with Your perfect will. I love you, Lord.

Think About It:
- What stumps (hidden hurts, secret sins, unforgiven attitudes) are buried in your heart?
- Are there attitudes that you need God's help to remove?

Finding Grace to Deal with Ants

Wherefore seeing we also are compassed about with so great a cloud of witnesses, let us lay aside every weight, and the sin which doth so easily beset us, and let us run with patience the race that is set before us,
—Hebrews 12:1

I parked my chair outside in the morning shade to enjoy the light breeze. Morning birds were serenading, and the summer flowers were in full bloom around me. I had my Bible, my journal, my cup of coffee, and I was set. Or so I thought.

I did not plant myself near an ant bed; I know how insidious they are. Nor did I attempt to disturb any creature. I was just seeking a few minutes of quiet under the summer blue sky. I was ready to commune with God.

But the ants found me. One crawled right across Ephesians. When I flicked him off, another crept onto my arm. Soon they arrived so frequently that I could not concentrate on the reading. Disgusted, I went inside, defeated by the ants.

Those ants had a lesson for me.

Unlike David in the Bible, I don't fight many giants that look like Goliath. Some of my giants crawl around on six legs and interrupt my Bible study. My other giants also resemble ants, and they often challenge and threaten to defeat me.

Ants – the little irritations and inconveniences that set my mind on me rather than on God.

Ants – the attitudes of self-reliance and apathy that like to attach themselves to my heart.

Ants – hurts and unforgiveness that run right across my soul when I am trying to love and serve God.

Ants – busy distractions that dim my vision and clutter my mind.

Ants – the insidious worries that attack my faith and peace.

Ants – the feelings of apathy that overtake me when I least expect them.

Ants. I don't seek them out, but they find me. Every. Day.

I don't have a spray that will chase the ants away from my heart and life, but God has given me His encouragement in His word. When I humble myself before Him and focus on Him, the ants are not as troublesome.

God gives me His grace to deal with the ants the ants so that I can live victoriously in Him. God is ready to help with the ants in your life if you ask Him.

Father, thank You for Your constant care and thank You for cleansing me from the sins that can so easily overtake me in this life. Keep me aware of the ants that are so prone to interrupt my time and relationship with You. Let your Holy Spirit empower me to overcome them. Thank You for being my Redeemer.

Think About It:
- What distractions are the most difficult for you to deal with in your walk with God?
- How can you minimize those distractions?

Me:
A Showcase of His Grace

I will praise thee; for I am fearfully and wonderfully made: marvelous are thy works; and that my soul knoweth right well.
—Psalm 139:14

I remember a quote from a plaque that I had when I was a teenager. "What you are is God's gift to you; what you make of yourself is your gift to God."—attributed to Hans Urs von Balthasar[3]

I thought about that quote a lot during my years in school. Recently, after reading 1 Corinthians 7:17-24, I slightly altered the quote, "Who I am is God's gift to me; How I use this life to glorify God is my gift to Him."

We can get caught up in the "if-onlys" of this life.

If only I were smarter.

If only I were more beautiful.

If only I had more money.

If only I had been born in a different place or at a different time.

If only I were younger, or older.

If only I were married, or single, or taller, or thinner, or more athletic, or ...

Periodically, I find myself needing to remind myself: God does not make mistakes.

My position in this life—
    who my parents were,
    where I was born,
    my nationality,
    my basic personality,
    my talents, my tendencies—
It is not a mistake.

God fashioned me to be me for His glory. I am perfectly planned.

The place where God has called and placed me is not an oversight. I am purposefully placed.

This life, this time, this place is my platform of praise—
> not to be dismissed or decried,
> but to be celebrated in its opportunities to showcase
> Who God is and what HE can do.

My life, today, just as it is, in all its messiness, is an opportunity to showcase the grace and love of God.

He knows that it is not how I start but how I finish that matters. I pray that today He will help me to be faithful.

Father, Lord, work in my life today and every day to make me a showcase of Your grace. Remind me that I am not a mistake. I am Your creation, designed for Your purpose, placed specifically and specially for Your work, Your pleasure, and Your glory. Strengthen me to be faithful each day in who You have created me to be and to remember that it is not how I started but how I finish that matters. Grow me to be more like Your Son, Jesus, for then I will be the best me I can be.

Think About It:
- Do you find it difficult to accept who God has created you to be?
- What can you thank God for each day about who you are?

Grace for Everyday Obedience

He hath shewed thee, O man, what is good; and what doth the Lord require of thee, but to do justly, and to love mercy, and to walk humbly with thy God?
—Micah 6:8

Things happen when we walk forward in obedience to God.

We want a warranty or a guarantee before we move, but God calls us to step out in faith. We want the end result; God asks us to trust Him with the final product. When we are busy obeying Him, He works.

This is the picture we see in the story of the ten lepers in Luke 17:12-19.

Jesus was on His way to Jerusalem, and on the way, He passed through Samaria and Galilee. He entered a village there, and ten lepers were standing away from the crowd. They cried to Him for mercy.

Jesus heard them, but He did not immediately heal them or promise them healing. Instead, He gave them a task.

"And when he saw them, he said unto them, Go shew yourselves unto the priests" (Luke 17:14).

Jesus could have spoken right then and healed them, but that is not what happened. They could have questioned Him, asked Him to give them something else to do, but they did not. They set out to see the priests, and a miracle occurred.

"And it came to pass, that, as they went, they were cleansed" (Luke 17:14).

Do you see that? *"As they went"*. They acted in obedience, and Jesus healed them as they went.

There is more to this story, so I hope you read it for yourself, but I want to focus on that phrase *"as they went"*.

Christ followers are tasked with obedience, even when it does not make sense to our human minds. We are tasked with obedience to God, even when we do not see immediate results.

God works in my obedience.

He has called me to be kind, though others may not be.

He has called me to trust Him when darkness is all around.

He has called me to continue in prayer when I don't see an answer.

He has called me to go and tell, to be a light, even when I may not see the fruit I expect.

Joshua and the Israelites marched around Jericho for seven days before they saw any action. Noah worked on the ark for 120 years without a convert. David hid in caves for long seasons before he was finally able to claim his rightful place as king. Abraham was almost one hundred years old before Isaac, the son of promise, was born.

God's timetable is not mine, and I am not in charge of the outcomes (sometimes this is hard for me to accept).

God has called me to faithfully walk His way in obedience to His word, knowing that He loves me and will bring His best to pass.

Every day, I face situations I do not understand and trials that are not comfortable. I do not have to fix every problem; I am called to obey God, one step, one moment at a time.

Obedience—it's a full-time job for me.

As I obey, God will do the work in me, in hearts, in lives, in the world.

I can trust Him with that.

By the way, I bet those lepers were glad they obeyed. We will be too.

Father, You are so good to me. Each day You are working in my life, even when I cannot trace Your hand. I know this. Help me to always trust You, to wait on You, as I continue to obey what You have called me to do. My job is to follow You. It is Your job to accomplish Your purposes. Thank You for being faithful to do just that. In Jesus' name I pray.

Think About It:
- Is there something that God is asking you to do?
- In what way do you need to trust Him?

Grace for the Martha Souls

Thou wilt shew me the path of life: in thy presence is fulness of joy; at thy right hand there are pleasures for evermore.
—Psalm 16:11

My name is Mary, but I have a Martha soul.

You know Martha. She, her sister Mary, and her brother Lazarus were close friends of Jesus. He ate with them and fellowshipped at their home in Bethany.

That is where Martha was in her element. She believed in work, in serving, in staying busy. No lollygagging around for her. So ingrained was her work ethic (we take pride in calling our busyness that) that she was known for reprimanding her sister, Mary, for not meeting her (Martha's) work quota.

In Luke 10, we find this description of Martha:

> Now it came to pass, as they went, that He entered into a certain village: and a certain woman named Martha received Him into her house. And she had a sister called Mary, which also sat at Jesus' feet, and heard His word. But Martha was cumbered about much serving, and came to Him, and said, Lord, dost thou not care that my sister hath left me to serve alone? bid her therefore that she help me (Luke 10:38–40).

Jesus had come to visit, and Martha was pulling out all the stops. Had Bethany been in southern Israel, there would have been fried chicken, mashed potatoes, greens, cornbread, and biscuits. Her apron would have been flapping, and the drops of perspiration would have been seen on her forehead as she rushed about checking on all the preparations, but I digress. I'm not sure what Martha was preparing, but she was busy with the work. She was busy serving. She was so busy that she did not have time to sit down with Jesus. Hmmm.

Mary, on the other hand, sat at Jesus' feet and listened. She relished and enjoyed His presence.

Martha was appalled. There was work to do! People to feed! How could Mary just ignore her efforts?

I believe that all the love of Jesus' heart was in the answer He gave in response to Martha's cry for her sister's help. "And Jesus answered and said unto her, Martha, Martha, thou art careful and troubled about many things: But one thing is needful: and Mary hath chosen that good part, which shall not be taken away from her" (Luke 10:41–42).

I never, ever read His words in these verses without feeling His longing for fellowship, for companionship, for a listening heart. And I am convicted.

I can find 1,001 things to do instead of praying. I'm not talking about sinful activities; I'm talking about service.

"The dishes need to be put away. Oh, let me get the baby for you. I will be happy to keep the nursery and teach and sing in the choir. Let me work in the kitchen, please! I think I'd better call and check on ..." You get the picture.

I can be so busy with many things that I miss the best thing—Jesus.

I'm not saying that it isn't important to serve. Thank God for the Christians with servant hearts whom God uses in ministry and life! But, if the service becomes the goal to attain instead of the response to Jesus' love, I have missed the most important part.

When my mom was alive, I spent many days at her house cleaning for her. I would rush between work, church, and family responsibilities, working like a whirlwind to be sure the bathroom was clean, the refrigerator organized, and the floors mopped. I wanted to do it for her. One day, though, she looked at me and said, "I wish you would just sit down and talk to me for a while. The house will wait."

I didn't fully understand then, but I think I do now. The service was good, but she wanted the fellowship. She wanted time with her child.

Sounds kind of like Jesus, doesn't it?

I won't lie. I still struggle with the busy part. I still try to validate my time by accomplishing things. I still like to check off my checklist. Some days I have trouble relishing His presence while the dishes wait in the sink.

I hope I am learning, though, to spend time in His presence before I start the work. I hope I am getting better at spending my energy on the most important, the good part that cannot be taken from me.

I hope that Jesus finds me at His feet listening to His words and smiles.

Father, forgive my busyness. Remind me that I can accomplish so much more when I work with You rather than for You. Remind me that my burnout comes when I am striving rather than resting in Your presence. Your presence is so, so good, Lord. Let me sit a while with You. In Jesus' name I pray.

Think About It:
- How hard is it for you to sit in Jesus' presence?
- Do you have a time set aside to spend with Him?

Unable:
And Then There Was Grace

O wretched man that I am! Who shall deliver me from the body of this death? I thank God through Jesus Christ our Lord.
—Romans 7:24-25

I am completely unable to live as a Christian.

The harder I try, the more I battle the frantic actions, empty words, defeated attitude, and my all-around imperfect state. My life is a sham, a pretense of good, covering a heart in great need of mercy and grace.

I long to be real, to love, to serve, but I am caught in a vicious battle with my own thoughts and selfish needs. My smile feels pasted on – my heart like lead. I go through the motions, but some days the struggle outweighs the joy.

Thank God!

I am in good company. The Apostle Paul in the seventh chapter of Romans also realized the futility of trying to live the Christian life in his own strength. He realized that grace was needed not only for salvation but for everyday living. The need for our Savior is a daily need.

So, thank God that the Christian life is more than I can do! It is His life, not mine. My strength is insufficient, but His strength is made perfect in weakness. My love is selfish, but His love reaches out and lifts me up.

When I try to operate in my own strength my focus is all wrong. I am not the generator, but the conduit; not the spring, but the riverbed; not the water, but the vessel.

Christ is the Life in me—the strength in me.

God did not leave me with an impossible task. He only asks that I allow Him to do the impossible through me.

The responsibility is His, the life is His, the strength is His. My only task is to yield—everything, every day—to Him.

Difficult? Some days it is. I struggle to give the control to Him. My human nature still grabs for the steering wheel of my life.

Impossible? No. As I grow closer to Him, I am learning to rest in Him, to let His life flow through me, to allow Him to carry the care.

Rewarding? It is the best life. The abundant life that He promised.

Father God, thank You for sending Jesus to save me from my sin, to deliver me from the darkness of death and destruction. Thank You for the grace of salvation. And thank You for the grace that lives in me and through me, that wraps around me and allows me to live for You each and every day. Help me to yield to this grace, to surrender my will to Yours so that I can live the abundant life that You have planned for me. You alone give me the strength to maneuver in the madness of this world. You alone shield me from the forces of my flesh that threaten to overcome me. Thank you for being my Savior and my King.

Think About It:
- Do you struggle to live as a Christian?
- What area or areas of your life do you need to surrender to Christ's control?

Grace for Eating Issues: Reading Your Bible

Wherefore laying aside all malice, and all guile, and hypocrisies, and envies, and all evil speakings, As newborn babes, desire the sincere milk of the word, that ye may grow thereby: If so be ye have tasted that the Lord is gracious.
—1 Peter 2:1-3

Feeding a premature infant is not for the faint of heart.

Our daughter's daughter entered the world five weeks early, weighing 5 pounds and 5 ounces. We were amazed at how perfect she was.

And then she promptly refused to eat.

According to the doctors and nurses, eating issues are a common malady for babies born at this gestational age, but it was not common for us. This little bit had three adults cajoling, tempting, cuddling, and loving around the clock as we tried to get enough nourishment into her little body. We went through multiple bottles and nipples and tried different formulas, but she was still losing weight.

Finally, or so it seemed to us, she was readmitted to the hospital and placed in the Neonatal Intensive Care Unit (NICU), where milk could be fortified, and where experts hovered and helped. It took a full week, but her weight began to turn around as she started eating normally. With a collective sigh of relief, we took her home again.

Sitting in a hospital room through the night gives one much time to think and pray. As I watched our little one, I thought about God's children. I thought about the nourishment needed for His children to grow into His likeness, and I thought about eating issues.

We have them, don't we?

In our world, God gives us many and varied opportunities to eat, but we still go days without feeding on His word. We have the scripture in our own language and preaching all around us. We have access to Bible study aids like commentaries and concordances. We have opportunities for Bible Study with other Christians, but we find them inconvenient or not to our liking.

So, we walk around as malnourished children, susceptible to all manner of spiritual illness. God's Holy Spirit cajoles and convicts, but we continue to fill our souls with the junk food offered by the world.

"I'm just too stressed to read the Bible."

"I can't concentrate right now."

"I'm too busy to meet with other Christians."

"The Bible is just too hard for me."

And we wonder why we have no spiritual strength, why trials overcome us and our faith falters.

Here is what I know, and our new granddaughter is a perfect example of this. We must eat to grow. "Faith comes by hearing, and hearing by the Word of God" (Romans 10:17).

Time in God's Word gives me:
- inner strength in time of trial
- calmness in times of stress
- hope when despair is raging
- a knowledge of God's presence and help
- peace that endures in a world of confusion and chaos
- a settled heart as I face each day.

There is no substitute for feasting on God's Word. There is no replacement for the spiritual food found there.

We tried multiple types of milk (formulas) with our granddaughter before she was able to eat well.

Here is a formula you might try as you feast on God's Word:

1. Choose a portion of scripture. It may be five verses or a chapter. I like to read through books of the Bible, a little each day.
2. Ask God to help you understand. His Holy Spirit is ready and willing to help.
3. Read the scripture and then read it again. No devotional book, blog, or commentary can take the place of reading God's Word for yourself.
4. Ask yourself:
   - What promises are in this passage?
   - What can I thank God for?
   - What commands are here for me to follow?
   - What new information do I see?
5. Pray and ask God to help you apply what you have read throughout the day.
6. It helps to have a small notebook to write in and a pencil to mark verses.

There is no better time to begin eating right than today, so today is a great day to begin reading God's Word.

"Study to shew thyself approved unto God, a workman that needeth not to be ashamed, rightly dividing the word of truth" (2 Timothy 2:15).

Father, what a privilege to have your word to read and study. You have written me a personal letter to guide me in this life. May I be faithful to read it daily, knowing You will help me understand, and You will give me the power to follow its teachings. How wonderful to read with the Author! Thank You for the comfort Your word gives. Forgive me for the times I have taken it for granted. In Jesus' name I pray.

Think About It:
- Do you have a set time to read your Bible?
- How do you study your Bible?

Grace to Pray Like David

My flesh and my heart faileth: but God is the strength of my heart, and my portion for ever.
—Psalm 73:26

Holed up in a cave, hiding from a vengeful king, David found himself overwhelmed with uncertainty and despair. (If you read the book of First Samuel, you will find that David fled to the caves on more than one occasion.) In this time of trial and persecution and desperation, what did David do?

He prayed.

Psalm 142 records the content of David's prayer from a cave. In this psalm, David poured out his complaint and his trouble before God. He agonized over his aloneness and the continued danger from King Saul. Like us, he had a few things that he wanted resolved.

But David did not stop there.

1. **David acknowledged God's understanding of his predicament** (verse 3). Even though the path was hard, David was assured that God knew the circumstances he faced.
2. **David claimed God as his refuge,** or place of safety (verse 5). David was in danger, but he still knew that God was his safe place.
3. **David claimed God as his portion** (verse 5). Though David had been anointed King of Israel, he could not take his rightful place because of Saul. David did not claim the throne as his portion. He claimed God as his portion. In doing that, he submitted to whatever God had for him.
4. **David looked forward to God's deliverance** (verse 7). David planned in advance to praise God for the deliverance He would accomplish. His faith was in God.

5. **David focused his heart on God's bountiful care** (verse 7). David was in trouble, but his heart was focused on God's care. He could rest there.

I can learn from David's prayer.
- Like David, sometimes I feel alone, dismayed, even frightened at the prospects ahead. God understands. I am His child, and He is not shaken when I carry my complaints and difficulties to Him. It helps just to know that He cares.
- No matter what is going on in this world, God is my refuge. I can go to Him. I can hide my heart in His love.
- Knowing that God is my portion keeps me from depending on this world to meet all my needs. The God of the Universe holds me, and that is enough.
- Times may be difficult now, but deliverance is coming. God will keep His promises. My hope is in Him.
- David focused on God's bountiful care. I can, too. My situation may not be what I want right now, but God is still caring for and providing for me. Thanking Him for daily grace keeps gratitude as my attitude.

Sometimes we want to think that the world has never been this bad before, but God's people have always suffered trials and persecutions. We are no exception. God's grace is sufficient to carry us through times of uncertainty and horror.

We can go to Him in prayer, and we, like David, can say with confidence, "He is my refuge and my portion."

Don't allow the darkness of the world to dim the light of His grace in your heart. Pray like David. He kept David. He can wrap you in His grace today as well.

Father, I thank You for the privilege of prayer and the examples of prayer that You have given me in Your word. Thank You for hearing when I run to You in confusion and despair. Thank You for comforting my heart in times of trouble. You are my strength and my shield, my portion forever. Thank You for providing for me and giving me grace for every day. Let me heart rest in Your care as I wait for You to work Your will in my life. In Jesus' precious name I pray.

Think About It:
- Is there something that you need to carry to God in prayer?
- Are you confident that God hears when you pray?
- How can you pray like David?

Grace When Passing Through

When thou passest through the waters, I will be with thee; and through the rivers, they shall not overflow thee: when thou walkest through the fire, thou shalt not be burned; neither shall the flame kindle upon thee. For I am the Lord thy God, the Holy One of Israel, thy Saviour:
—Isaiah 43:2–3

A marvelous truth lies in the first three verses of Isaiah 43. Actually, there are several great truths, but one has captured my heart.

As a child of God, I am passing through.

In these verses, God is clear about the reality of trials and troubles for His children; He does not promise to remove them. He doesn't say, "If you pass through the fire"; He says, "When you pass through the fire." Tribulation in this life is certain.

The floods will come. The waters will flow. The fire will blaze.

The glorious truth, however, is that I will PASS THROUGH all of this. I will pass through, and I will emerge whole on the other side.

In that truth lies the power and victory for my life. I may be sloshing in the mud of living. I may smell the smoke and feel the heat of the flames, but I am passing through unharmed.

This life is not taking me down.

Herein lies the essence of biblical hope—the assurance that God has this, that God has me!

I can keep walking. I can keep swimming. I can keep brushing away the ashes, because I know—I know—I will pass through this, whatever this is.

He is the Lord.

He is my Savior (Isaiah 43:3).

I am precious in His sight (Isaiah 43:4).

He is with me (Isaiah 43:5),
and I will pass through!

Whatever you are facing today, if you are a child of God, you will pass through it. God has promised, and He is always faithful to do what He says.

> God is our refuge and strength, a very present help in trouble. Therefore will not we fear, though the earth be removed, and though the mountains be carried into the midst of the sea; Though the waters thereof roar and be troubled, though the mountains shake with the swelling thereof (Psalm 46:1–3).

Father, I thank You for Your precious promises. I thank You for being with me in the fire and in the flood. I don't like the trials, Lord, but I love that You are always with me. That I am never alone. This life is not easy, and sometimes the trials seem to pile up. But You, Lord, You give victory in Your presence. Remind me that this life is not eternal, but You are. This life is not all there is, but You are. Help me to stay focused on the Truth of You, for You are Truth. In Jesus' name.

Think About It:
- How does knowing that you will pass through the trial help you during the trial?
- How does knowing that God is always with you strengthen you?
- Does God's presence mean that things will always work out the way that you want them to?

Today

Today, when you face
the struggles of the day
and your faith, which seemed so strong
just slowly fades away.
Remember I am near,
Through Me, you'll persevere.
In My presence
you will find My strength.

Today, when the fight
takes more than you can give,
and you want to quit and run
before the day's begun.
Remember that I fought
the battle just for you.
In My presence
you will find My peace.

Today, when life's grief
Weighs heavy on your soul
and the burdens that you bear
are beyond what you control.
Remember I am here,
lean into My embrace.
In My presence
you will find My grace.

Dare to Be a Daniel

Wherefore take unto you the whole armor of God, that ye may be able to withstand in the evil day, and having done all, to stand.
—Ephesians 6:23

On page 322 in the old Broadman Hymnal, is a children's song called "Dare to Be a Daniel". The refrain goes like this:

> *Dare to be a Daniel*
> *Dare to stand alone*
> *Dare to have a purpose firm*
> *Dare to make it known (Philip Bliss)*[4]

Today is a good day to be a Daniel.

Daniel's story is recorded in the Old Testament. Just an adolescent when Jerusalem was invaded and destroyed by Nebuchadnezzar's army, he lived the rest of his life in the city of Babylon in the service of pagan rulers.

A young Jewish boy, stolen, enslaved, challenged by excess and debauchery, alone—certainly not an auspicious beginning or an ideal life. How did he survive? His childhood was interrupted by horror, but he stood firm in his resolve to honor the King of Kings.

He served with grace and wisdom. He lived with integrity. His accusers had to attack his loyalty to God to find any fault in him.

How did Daniel stay true to God?

Four principles of his life stand out as I read through the book of Daniel.

1. **Daniel purposed in his heart (Daniel 1:8).** Before any temptation was put in front of Daniel, he had already made his decision—he would remain true, no matter what. He did not leave an escape

hatch in case a more pleasant choice appeared; his will was set. We often underestimate the power of our will. When we determine or purpose to do a thing, we set the stage to accomplish that purpose. Daniel's heart and will were set.
2. **Daniel spoke truth (Daniel 4:19-27).** Even in the face of danger, Daniel spoke God's truth. The message was not always pleasant or popular, but he accurately relayed what God said.
3. **Daniel stood firm when opposed and threatened (Daniel 6:5).** When schemed against and threatened, Daniel simply continued doing what was right. He trusted God for the outcome, always realizing that his life was in God's hands. I do not sense frantic unease or ranting as I read through the book of Daniel. Instead, I see him quietly doing his job in the very presence of evil.
4. **Daniel praised God and gave Him the credit and glory (Daniel 2:19-23).** Praise permeates the book of Daniel. Daniel was not in a good place, but he served a good God—and he let this be known. When he interpreted a dream, he gave God the glory. He told Nebuchadnezzar that his kingdom existed at God's pleasure, not because of his own ability. Daniel consistently stopped to pray three times each day—his life a consistent witness of his dependence on God.

I can learn from Daniel today:
- **I have decided to follow Jesus!** Just as Daniel purposed in his heart, I must purpose in mine. What I determine in my heart to do and be matters. The choice cannot be left to a chance moment. My heart must be fixed on God's desire and God's plan.
- **I will speak God's truth.** In a world that sensationalizes lies and deceit, my words must accurately repeat and reflect what God has said. My opinions do not matter so much. God's truth reigns.

- **I must stand firm.** When trials come and persecutions arise, I must stand in God's strength and in the truth of Who He is—not frantic but trusting in His sovereign will.
- **God gets the glory—all the glory.** He alone is worthy of praise, and it is my job to offer it to Him.

Father, just like in Daniel's day, this world can be pretty scary. Grant me the strength to stand strong in Your truth, to speak Your truth, to follow You in complete obedience, and to always give You the praise for the work that is done. Help me to follow Daniel's example to be a faithful servant for You. I love you, Lord.

Think About It:
- Is there a place in your life where you need to take a stand or speak truth?
- Does God receive the glory for the good things that happen in your life?

Five Principles of Praise

While I live will I praise the Lord: I will sing praises unto my God while I have any being.
—Psalm 146:2

Praise is not the norm today.

We are critical and judgmental. Our thoughts and, therefore, our words automatically turn to the "what's wrong" rather than "what's right" topics. We have been primed to see the negative and to blame someone for it. Not willing to be caught off guard, we attempt to spot the trouble before it spots us.

A person who focuses on good may seem a little abnormal, but abnormal can be a good thing.

Praise has power.

Throughout scripture, we are commanded (yes, I did say commanded) to praise the Lord, to give thanks, to be thankful people (Read Psalm 150). These commands, when obeyed, force our minds to focus on the multitude of blessings in our lives. Praise does not ignore the problems, but it does recognize that God is more than the problems. Praise and thanksgiving remind the heart that the morning newscast is not the final word for the day.

Praise calls us beyond ourselves to see the power and the beauty and the love and the grace of God.

A quick perusal of scripture gives us example after example of the importance of praise. Here are just a few:

We praise based on Who God is. While many times we praise God for things that He has done or good things in our lives, our goal is to praise His innate character and being. Things do not always go the way we want them to in this life, but God is ALWAYS good, and merciful, and kind, and full of grace.

- "Because thy lovingkindness is better than life, my lips shall praise thee" (Psalm 63:3).
- "For the Lord is great, and greatly to be praised" (Psalm 96:4).
- "For his merciful kindness is great toward us: and the truth of the Lord endures forever. Praise ye the Lord" (Psalm 117:2).

Praise is a full-time job. Psalm 113:3 tells us to praise God from sunrise to sunset. Psalm 145:2 encourages us to praise Him every day forever and ever, and Psalm 119:62 has us rising at midnight to give thanks to God. I believe that is what Paul and Silas did when they were in the Philippian jail (Acts 16).

Praising God is a sign of a fixed, or stable, heart (Psalm 108:1), and it is an **antidote to fear** (Psalm 56:4). The verses in the fourth chapter of Philippians remind us to keep an attitude of thanksgiving as we take our cares to the Lord. "Be careful for (anxious about) nothing; but in everything by prayer and supplication with thanksgiving let your requests be made known unto God. And the peace of God, which passes all understanding, shall keep your hearts and minds through Christ Jesus" (Philippians 4:6–7).

Praise is a sacrifice (Hebrews 13:15, Psalm 116:17). This is because praise forces us to step away from our focus on the world and on the problem and set our eyes on God. Praise does not come naturally to us, but it results from our choice to trust God rather than the situation. This is hard, but this is a sacrifice that we offer to our Lord.

Praise is a sign of life. Psalm 115:17 tells us that the dead do not praise God, and in Isaiah 38:19, the prophet says the living praise God. If we can find nothing for which to praise God, we should probably check our spiritual life. "While I live will I praise the Lord: I will sing praises unto my God while I have any being" (Psalm 146:2).

These are just a few of the many principles about praise in the Bible. You may want to spend some time doing your own search. Or perhaps, now is a good time just to praise Him.

Father, I do praise You for who You are and for all that You do. You are the mighty God and the King of Kings and yet You choose to care for me each and every day. Thank You for providing for me and carrying me through this life. You are a good Father, and You are worthy to be praised. Today, I lift my heart and life in praise to You.

Think About It:
- When you pray, do you spend time praising God?
- Which one of the principles of praise was the most surprising to you?

Grace Under the Refrigerator

If we confess our sins, he is faithful and just to forgive us our sins, and to cleanse us from all unrighteousness.
—1 John 1:9

That ball rolled right under the... refrigerator. I did not want to go there this morning, but it was the baby's ball.

I found a flashlight, got down on all fours, and shined the light into the darkness. There was the ball—sitting right in the middle of a dusty mess!

If you ask me if I make my bed every morning, I can go super spiritual on you and righteously proclaim, "Yes". If you walk into my house, you will see it is neat and appears clean.

But under that refrigerator—don't go there!

I did go there this morning, though, for the sake of the baby's ball. You know what I found? Dirt, dust, and other things that I won't mention. That spot was clean when we placed that refrigerator there, but just look what living life has brought in!

And so began a morning of cleaning.

My heart is like that.

I can clean up my actions on the outside and look pretty good, but life happens. Interactions occur. Problems arise. I rub up against attitudes and actions that bother me.

Thoughts, grievances, hurts, pride, you name it, lodge in my heart and leave it less than pristine. Dusty places in my life that I have not allowed God's light to shine on can make my heart a mess.

Sometimes, a word or a look will land right in the middle of one of those dusty places, and that dirt will become evident in my response.

I have a choice then. Acknowledge the dirt and allow God to cleanse it, or close my eyes and leave the dirt to continue collecting the dust bunnies of a bad attitude.

The good news is that when I acknowledge my sin—my heart mess—to God, He is faithful and just to clean it up (1 John 1:9). He cleans from the inside out, so there is no worry about being surprised by a mess when God is in charge.

I think that ball rolled under my refrigerator for a reason. Today is probably a good day to allow God to do some cleaning in my heart.

"Create in me a clean heart, O God; and renew a right spirit within me" (Psalm 51:10).

Father, clean out my heart today. Shine the flashlight of Your love into all the dark crevices and root out the attitudes and sins that are hiding there. Make me clean, Lord. Forgive me for allowing wrong thoughts to build up. I confess them to You. Thank you for cleansing me today.

Think About It:
- Are there things in your heart that need to be confessed to God?
- Is today a good day to pray Psalm 51:10?

Grace Gives Us Glad Songs

I will sing unto the Lord as long as I live: I will sing praise to my God while I have my being. My meditation of Him shall be sweet: I will be glad in the Lord.
—Psalm 104:33-34

God is intimately involved with His creation. Psalm 104 tells us this.

The rhythms of life that we observe were planned and created by Him. From the foundation of the Earth to the heavens above and to the smallest particle of life in the deepest ocean, God's intricate design and care are evident.

He designed the seasons and the paths for the moon and stars. He conceived the instincts that guide the behavior of the animals in the forests, jungles, and deserts. His ongoing care maintains the forces that support life and growth in this world.

Knowing this gives me reason to praise Him regardless of what may be happening in my life right now. I can choose to praise Him for who He is and for what He has already done.

So, what shall I praise God for today? I will praise Him for:
- the rays of sunlight just topping the trees
- the song of the cardinal ringing through the morning
- the misty air left over from a nighttime rain
- the smile of the stranger I pass
- the warm cup of coffee in my hand
- the butterfly darting past
- the breath in my lungs
- the cluck of the chickens looking for bugs
- the smell of rain in the air

- the colors of the clouds in the sky
- the antics of the kitten on the lawn
- the rhythm of the changing moon
- the breath of breeze in the evening.
- the magnificence of His grace that saves and keeps me.

I shall praise Him for Who He is and for His marvelous creation.
I will stand in awe of His love and care.
I will be glad in the Lord.
"O Lord, how manifold are thy works! in wisdom hast thou made them all: the earth is full of thy riches" (Psalm 104:24).

Father, I am glad today. Glad that You are my Father. Glad that I live in this world You created. I know that mankind has misused so much of it, but I still walk in Your care. I praise You today for Your mighty works, for Your amazing creativity, for Your beauty which You have spread across Your creation, for Your loving care, for Your abundant provision. Just saying these words of praise lifts my heart even more. You are good, Father. You are so, so good. You make my soul rejoice.

Think About It:
- What can you praise God for today?
- What makes your heart glad?
- Make a list of God's wonderful works. Spend some time thanking Him for all He has done.

Five Smooth Stones for Today

For so is the will of God, that with well doing ye may put to silence the ignorance of foolish men: As free, and not using your liberty for a cloak of maliciousness, but as the servants of God. Honor all men. Love the brotherhood. Fear God. Honor the king.
—1 Peter 2:15-17

Lord, You have said that Your throne is established from old and You are from everlasting (Psalm 94:2). I do not really understand that word everlasting. I accept by faith that You have always been, and You always will be, but Your eternalness is beyond my comprehension.

I am stuck in the now. I know the date of my birth, though I don't remember that day. I know death will come, but I do not know when.

And here I am today, standing on this pinprick of eternity, wondering.

I wonder at Your majesty and strength. I wonder at Your holiness. I wonder at Your creation, and my heart is drawn by a silent voice telling me this is not my home.

This world is flooded with evil, and its shouts and rampages seem to shake the very earth. You, though, have said "the world also is established, that it cannot be moved" (Psalm 94:1).

The flood of evil is rising and crashing into my now, but You are, "mightier than the noise of many waters, yes, than the mighty waves of the sea" (Psalm 94:4).

Sometimes I feel like David facing the giant, Goliath. The situation seems hopeless as the Goliath of evil accuses and attacks.

You called David to stand, and You have called me to stand as well (Ephesians 6:13).

When David went out to confront Goliath, he picked up five smooth stones to use against the giant. I think about what You have given me in the battle that I face.

When I face my giants, I pick up:
- The Word of God
- Prayer
- Obedience to your word
- Love for God
- Love for Others

These are the five smooth stones which I have today. As I stand in Your strength, may I wield them wisely and well to counteract and neutralize the voice of the enemy, remembering that all I do and all I am is for Your glory. May I faithfully study Your word and obey it, so that I will have a sharp sword to use when the enemy attacks. Let my heart stay constantly in tune with You so that You can love others through me and guide me in the way I should go. You are my fortress and deliverer. You will not fail.

Think About It:
- How does God's word help you in the struggles you face in this life?
- How much do you depend on prayer?
- Do you consider loving God and loving other stones to use against the enemy? Why or why not?

Grace to Remember

But these things have I told you, that when the time shall come, ye may remember that I told you of them. And these things I said not unto you at the beginning, because I was with you.
—John 16:4

I forget a lot these days.

I walk into a room and circle fruitlessly as I try to remember why I entered.

I see an old acquaintance, and I must go through the entire database in my head to try and pull out the name.

I make lists to organize my thinking, and I lose them.

Forgetting is my new talent.

Psalm 77, though, talks about remembering. The psalmist communicates things that are remembered—important things.

When there was trouble, *he remembered God* (verse 3). The psalmist remembered God's law and he was troubled. His spirit was overwhelmed.

I feel that way sometimes. When I think of my own sinfulness, I am overwhelmed by the magnitude of what it took for God to save me. I remember Him, though, and I am so thankful for all He has done for me.

That is not all the psalmist remembered. In verse six, *he remembered his song in the night.* You know who gives songs in the night—those times of hope and joy in the middle of trial and trouble? According to Job 35:10, God does.

God is my song leader and the One Who sings to my heart when it needs comfort. I can remember God's song for me, even when the music of the world shouts despair.

The psalmist also *remembered the times of God's blessing* (Psalm 77:10). When the world seems to be falling apart, remembrances of God's steadfast love and care are important. Sometimes I need to just sit and think about how God has kept me in the past to help me know He will keep me in the future.

Finally, the psalmist *remembered the works of the Lord and His wonders of old* (verse 11). God had led Israel through the sea and through the wilderness. He had provided for their every need. He had cleared the way to the promised land. God had been faithful. David remembered God's faithfulness.

God has kept me through illness and hardship. He has comforted me during times of deep sorrow, and He has cared for my soul when others turned away. He has always been faithful.

When I look around at the wonders of this Earth, I know that God is able. I see Him in the tiniest insect and in the giant elephant. I am awed by His creative goodness that is evidenced in the flowers and landscapes and creatures and stars and sunrises. I know He is a mighty God. When I struggle with discouragement, I must remember. The God of angel armies is also the God who cares for the lilies and the birds. He has assured me that He cares for me even more than them (Matthew 6:25-30).

There are two things in Psalm 77 that the psalmist does because of his remembering. Look at verse 12, "I will meditate also of all thy work and talk of thy doings."

1. The psalmist thinks about God's work, and
2. He talks about what God is doing.

That sounds so simple, but what we think about and talk about certainly impacts our well-being. I think the psalmist knew the key to maintaining an attitude of faith.

So, I may forget where I put my keys and may not be able to find my car in the parking lot, but there are some important things I am going to remember.
- I will remember God.
- I will remember His times of blessing.
- I will remember His works.
- I will remember His songs in the night and what He has done in the past.

I will think about these things, and I will talk about these things with others.

In fact, I believe I will put these on my "to-do" list for today, if I can just find that "to-do" list.

Father, You have been so good to me. I remember how You have kept me and comforted me. I know that You have brought me through trials and temptations so many times. You have provided when I didn't see how there was a way. Help me to always remember. And keep these testimonies on my lips, Lord, to encourage others in their walk. It's a dark world out there. We need to always be thinking about and talking about You. In Jesus' sweet name I pray.

Think About It:
- What are some blessings that you remember God has done for you?
- Who can you tell about what God has done?

Grace to Cast Your Care on God

Come unto me, all ye that labor and are heavy laden, and I will give you rest. Take my yoke upon you, and learn of me; for I am meek and lowly in heart: and ye shall find rest unto your souls. For my yoke is easy, and my burden is light.
—Matthew 11:28-30

When my husband took up fly fishing several years ago, he began to practice casting. He set up his fly pole with the proper line and leader, and before he ever went to the water, he stood in the yard and practiced his cast over and over again. He watched videos of the experts and made sure he held the rod correctly. He talked to experienced fly fishermen. And he practiced.

He can cast with the best of them now, and fly fishing is his fun hobby.

I thought about his experience with casting as I read 1 Peter 5:7 recently, "Casting all your care upon Him (God), for He careth for you."

It hit me that I am not very good at casting my cares on God. I have read and talked about that verse all my life. I have quoted it to others many times.

But I don't think I have practiced it like my husband practices casting his line for fly fishing.

Peter was referencing Psalm 55:22 when he wrote this verse, "Cast thy burden upon the Lord, and he shall sustain thee: he shall never suffer the righteous to be moved."

The word "casting" in 1 Peter means to throw something upon and leave it, like throwing a saddle on a horse. You don't throw a saddle on a horse and then take it off and put it on your own back.

But unfortunately, that is the picture when I pray about a worry and then continue to carry the burden in my heart. It's like I believe that I can solve the problem better than God can. There seems to be some hidden pride wrapped up in there somewhere.

Verse seven in 1 Peter five builds on verse six, which instructs me to humble myself before God. Before I can trust Him with my care, I must admit that I am completely unable to solve the problems myself. **I need Him**. I must humble myself before Him.

As I read these verses and meditated on them, I confessed my lack of faith and my prideful spirit, and I began practicing my casting. I have a whole list of cares that I am working on placing in my Father's hands and leaving there. I'm sure that I won't master this skill all at once, but with His help, I'm determined to trust Him with my concerns. And, as a friend reminded me, when I cast them there in faith, I will thank Him for receiving and caring for them. Because He cares for me. Perhaps you have a list you need to practice casting, too.

Oh Father, how silly of me to think that I can carry these burdens alone. You never intended me to be my own burden bearer. You never intended for me to be loaded down with the cares of the world. You have called me to come to You and share the yoke with You. When I do that, the burden is light because You carry it. Forgive my foolish pride in trying to do it all myself. I need You, Lord. How I need You. Thank You for being willing to carry me. Thank You for wrapping me in Your precious grace each day. In Jesus' name I pray.

Think About It:
- How often do you continue to fret about the things that you carry to God in prayer?
- Can you make a list of cares that you can cast on Him?
- Can you leave them with Him by thanking Him for taking care of them each time you think of them?

Grace to Follow Hard After God

My soul followeth hard after thee: thy right hand upholdeth me.
—Psalm 63:8

We had this beagle named Freckles.

Freckles was a great dog. She nurtured kittens and visited neighbors. She played with growing toddlers and searched for lost bunnies. She nuzzled her way right into the heart of our family.

But Freckles' great love was trailing. She would periodically escape the confines of the yard and take off on her own adventures through the woods. We would try to find her and bring her back, but all we could hear was her voice echoing her chase through the pines. She had caught the scent of a deer or some other interesting animal, and she was in her element. She might be ready to drop, tongue lolling, fur matted with burrs, but we could not deter her from her quest. She was all in.

When I read Psalm 63, I see Freckles' name where I have penciled it beside verse eight. That is because I see her when I read the words "followeth hard." She followed hard after anything she trailed.

David followed hard after God. Some Bible versions translate this as "cling to" or "follow close behind," but I like thinking of following hard after God. I understand that picture—thanks to our dog, Freckles.

What does it mean to follow hard after God? In this psalm, David praised God's lovingkindness and His help. He talked of thirsting for God as a traveler in the desert thirsts for water. He meditated on God. He praised God with joyful lips. He remembered how God had kept him, and David wanted to know God above all else.

When I truly get a glimpse of who God is, all else will pale in the light of His glory. Nothing—no. thing.—in this life will keep me from praising Him, from seeking Him, from finding joy in Him, from following Him. I will not be stopped.

Sometimes roadblocks pop up when I pursue God.
- Desire for comfort
- Pain
- My expectation that God will do things my way
- Persecution, which may look like ridicule or dismissal
- Busyness

When I pursue Him with my whole heart, however, I can move through painful circumstances because my eyes are fixed on the goal—HIM!

So, I want to be like Freckles following a scent. I want to follow hard after God. If you hear my voice raised in praise, just know I am on God's trail. I will not be stopped.

Jesus, when You return, I want to be found with my tongue lolling, matted with burrs, done in from following hard after You. I want to walk so close behind You that Your footprints are still warm when I place my feet in them. Help me not to be distracted by the things and cares of this world. Keep my focus on You alone. In Your precious name I pray.

Think About It:
- What distracts you from following God?
- How can you follow Him more closely today?

Grace for Hard Lessons

Watch ye and pray, lest ye enter into temptation. The spirit truly is ready, but the flesh is weak.
—Mark 14:38

In Luke 22:33, Peter made a declaration, "And he (Peter) said unto Him, Lord, I am ready to go with Thee, both into prison and to death."

I believe that as much as is humanly possible, Peter meant that.

He and the other disciples carried two swords with them (Luke 22:38) as they followed Jesus to the Garden of Gethsemane. Jesus knew about those swords.

But there in the garden, while Jesus agonized in prayer, they slept. Jesus had asked them to watch with him, but they were tired, and the flesh took over.

When the soldiers came and Judas stepped up to betray Jesus, Peter took one of those swords, and swung it. Evidently, the man he aimed at ducked, because he cut off the man's ear instead of his head (John 18:10). Jesus stopped Peter and told him to put the sword away. Then Jesus healed the man's ear.

I feel for Peter in these verses. He was in the right place at the right time. He wanted to protect Jesus, but he was operating under a faulty belief system.

Peter thought he had the situation covered. He believed he was "good to go." After all, he knew Jesus. He loved Jesus.

But that faulty belief system—the belief that centered in self—tripped him up.

He was confident in his own ability, so he failed to pray (Mark 14:37, 38).

He was secure in his own strength and stature, so he swung the sword.

He was intent on stopping the show, but Jesus stopped him.

What he thought would be his greatest victory crashed and burned. Peter left the garden defeated and confused, and he ended up denying Jesus. That was not what he planned.

I can point my finger at Peter, or I can realize that Peter's hard lesson is a lesson for me.

I have stepped out before without praying, confident in my own ability, and, like Peter, I have failed.

Peter could not do Kingdom work in his own strength, and neither can I.

I can shout about my commitment to Jesus, but if I am not clinging to Him every moment of every day, I will fail. I must pray and connect with the Source of all Strength. I must depend on His wisdom. I must follow His plan, even when it does not match my own. Wasn't that Jesus' prayer in the garden? "Not my will, but Thine be done" (Luke 22:42).

So, I do not tsk-tsk Peter's failure. My heart goes out to him, and I realize that I am just as vulnerable to failure as he was.

Only submission to the Holy Spirit and use of the full armor of God will get me through the pitfalls of this world. My sword is the Word of God, and I must study to be skilled in its use.

The moment that I think I've got this is the moment that my failure looms.

"Humble yourselves in the sight of the Lord, and he shall lift you up" (James 4:10).

Father, forgive me for the times I have run ahead of You, for the times I have assumed that I knew the best way without asking for Your guidance, for the times I have tried to depend on my own wisdom, which is really not wisdom at all. I submit to You, knowing that without You I can do nothing. Only as I abide in You will I bear fruit for You.

Keep me close, Jesus. I am so prone to acting without praying. I commit this moment, this day to You. In Jesus' name I pray.

Think About It:
- How often do you commit to a task without praying?
- What will help you remember to commit your work and play to the Lord?

Vitamins for the Soul

Then was our mouth filled with laughter, and our tongue with singing: then said they among the heathen, The Lord hath done great things for them.
—Psalm 126:2

Vitamins line the shelves of stores today and they are advertised relentlessly on every social media feed. There is always one that is better, one that is a cure-all for every disease.

I took some vitamins today, but they didn't come from the pharmacy or a shopping center. They were not shrink-wrapped (I hate that stuff) or rattling around in a box or bottle. I didn't even have to swallow them.

I saw them, heard them, and touched them, and they fed my soul.

As I put on my sneakers on the back porch, two owls were having a deep conversation in the woods behind the house. I stopped and listened, and my ears were fed.

During my early morning walk, the sun burst through the mist in glorious light. My eyes were fed.

I emailed some friends, and we laughed—virtually. My mind was nourished.

Breezes rippled through the day, swirling the clouds overhead, cooling the air, and stimulating my senses of sight and touch.

Psalm 24 told me about the coming of my King, and my heart was filled.

I bowed my head in prayer for my family and my friends and my nation and my world, and my soul was soothed and sustained.

God gives us vitamins to strengthen us every day and to build our immunity to fear and despair during times of crisis. Just like the vitamins that come in bottles, we must take them regularly for them to work well in our systems.

We can talk about our symptoms and rehash our troubles and focus on what we can't have or can't do. We can collapse with worry and sorrow. We can fret over the disarray and trouble in our lives and in the world. Or we can take our vitamins.

Every. Day.

Here are some of my favorite vitamins to try:
- Reading words of Scripture
- Talking with God
- Listening to the sounds of nature
- Relishing the beauty of God's creation
- Enjoying times of exercise
- Communicating with friends and relatives
- Singing and giving praise to God
- Giving thanks

Vitamins don't make diseases and troubles go away, but they can strengthen us to face them if we faithfully take them daily.

"I sought the Lord, and he heard me, and delivered me from all my fears" (Psalm 34:4).

Father, You have provided so many vitamins to strengthen us for our walk in this dark world. I thank You for giving us the resources we need to walk with You daily. Thank You for Your word and Your beautiful world. Thank You for brothers and sisters in Christ who walk this journey with us. Help me to faithfully take the vitamins You have provided for me, to use the resources You have given, so that I can live faithfully for You. I love You, Lord.

Think About It:
- What do you do when you are discouraged?
- Are there soul vitamins that you need to add to your daily routine? What are they?

Grace for the Struggle

Ye are all the children of light, and the children of the day: we are not of the night, nor of darkness.
—1 Thessalonians 5:5

The struggle is real, and it goes back to the beginning of time.

Back to Cain and Abel. Back to the Israelites and the Canaanites. Back to the early church. Back to Thessalonica.

The struggle—How does light live with darkness?

Paul knew that the darkness did not just go away. Evil is rampant and will continue until our Lord returns for His children. Paul spent chapter four of First Thessalonians comforting the church with the promise of the Lord's coming. What a glorious hope that is.

Still, Christians are here today. How do we maneuver through everyday life? How do we live in this sin-filled dark world? Paul gave some very clear advice in First Thessalonians chapter five.

First, remember who you are and whose you are. Christians are children of light. We do not belong to the darkness of this world. Don't believe the lies of the darkness; remember and believe the promises of God. We are to be aware and watchful.

Next, suit up with God's armor (1 Thessalonians 5:8). This is not the armor of the world. God offers the breastplate of faith and love and the helmet of salvation. We need not fear the wrath of God. Jesus Christ paid our sin debt in full, and Satan's host of darkness has no hold on the child of God.

Be who you were called to be (verses 11–15). This means we will live as God has called us to live. Honor Christian leaders. Love each other. Be at peace with each other. Encourage each other. Warn those who are difficult and lazy. Gently care for the weak. Be patient with all. Give back good for evil. In fact, chase what is good with all people. Trust me, this is a full-time job.

Rejoice (verse 16). This is not empty merry-making. Our rejoicing is in the Lord and in what He has done for us. There is always reason to rejoice in His goodness and grace.

Pray without ceasing (verse 17). As our world grows ever darker, our hearts must seek Him increasingly. Pray without ceasing is an instruction to breathe in and breathe out communication with our Father. We must stay connected to our Source.

In everything give thanks (verse 18). No matter the circumstances, no matter how dark it gets, continue to offer praise to the Father of Light for we are children of light. We praise Him for Who He is.

Quench not the Spirit (verse 19). We must not stifle the promptings of the very One Who guides our hearts through this darkness. We must follow Him.

Test all things, and cling to what is right (verse 21). Sometimes it is hard to discern what is right and what is wrong in this troubled world. That is when we must test our knowledge against scripture and through prayer. As God leads us, we must have courage to cling to what is right.

Abstain from all appearance of evil (verse 22). It is easy to compromise when everyone around is following darkness, but God has called us to stay in the light. Stand for truth.

This is just a summary of Paul's instructions to the church in Thessalonica, and it is a good list for me today. It seems a bit daunting when I read it, so I'm thankful that I am not on my own when it comes to following Christ. You see, obeying Christ is all about Him working through me rather than me following a list of rules. Paul makes this clear when he ends his instructions with

"And the very God of peace sanctify you wholly; and I pray God your whole spirit and soul and body be preserved blameless unto the coming of our Lord Jesus Christ. Faithful is he that calleth you, who also will do it" (1 Thessalonians 5:24).

We follow Him by walking in His light, but He is the one who will sanctify us, preserve us blameless, and faithfully do the work of good in us.

Thank God.

Oh Father, You have given me clear instructions for my journey through this world, but they are not easy instructions. They require the empowerment of your Holy Spirit working in my life every day. I yield my heart and life to You right now. Let me walk in Your Light and shine Your Light in this lost world. You are strong and mighty, God. You are able to keep me and lead me victoriously through the darkness. I trust You. In Jesus' precious name.

Think About It:
- Which of Paul's instructions seems most daunting to you?
- Which requires more study?
- What is your biggest struggle with the darkness in this world?

God Is

When the quilt of life unfolds
and I can't understand the intricacies and patterns
of my Father's plan,
He calls me to look beyond the circumstances I face
and live with confidence,
because I know
God is grace.

When the night of confusion falls
and my heart gropes to find and comprehend
the path of right,
He calls me to look beyond the blinding gloom
of this present darkness
and grasp that
God is light.

When the earthquake of sorrow shakes
the foundation of my soul,
and this world provides no shelter of relief,
He calls me by the steadfastness of His character
and the surety of His promises
to experience.
God is peace.

Grace Isn't Stagnant

He that believeth on me, as the scripture hath said, out of his belly shall flow rivers of living water.
—John 7:38

I learned the meaning of the word "stagnant" from my dad.

We were fishing close to a bridge, far out in the woods. The creek flowed deep under the bridge, carrying cool, clear water toward the river. Over beside the bridge, though, was a backwater—a place where water sometimes backed up when there was abundant rain. When the water level decreased, the water that ended up in the backwater had no exit point, meaning there was no flow.

So, the water just sat there, if water can sit.

When I saw the backwater, it was covered with green algae. There was a slight smell, not associated with the creek, that I soon learned came from the rotting vegetation caught in the still water.

I asked my dad about it. "That's a stagnant pool," he said. "We don't fish there. The life is in the flowing water."

I've never forgotten that picture or the explanation. "Life is in the flowing water."

Sometimes, I feel stagnant.

Every day, I take in blessings, provision, light, and love. God gives exceedingly abundantly above all that I can ask or think (Ephesians 3:20). He fills my life enough to overflow, but does it?

Does grace flow through my life, or do I hoard His love? Whom am I helping? Where am I sharing God's abundance and mercy? How am I showing His love?

If I take in and take in and take in without letting God's goodness flow out of me, I am in danger of becoming stagnant. Just like that backwater.

Have you ever met someone who claimed to be a Christian, but whose words were marked with bitterness and complaining? No joy or thankfulness was flowing out from the Living Water in their soul. Perhaps, you were seeing an example of a stagnant Christian.

I know that my salvation is not dependent on works. I also know, though, that this great salvation provided by grace to me through Jesus Christ results in good works. It is marked by peace and joy and hope, even in the darkness of this life. I am filled up with the grace of God, and I need to let the blessings out!

Perhaps this is some of the motivation behind Paul's statement, "woe unto me if I preach not the gospel" (I Corinthians 9:16). The Word was in him, and it needed to come out!

I need to share what God has done for me, or I risk stagnation.

Stagnant is not healthy or vibrant. Stagnant stinks!

The opposite of stagnant is living. Living water flows, refreshes, and gives life. Jeremiah 17:13 tells us that God is the fountain of living waters, and Jesus promised that when we believe in Him, Living Water will flow from us—refreshing, giving life (John 7:38).

For that water to flow, we must be connected to the fountain—the source—which is God.

I don't know about you, but I don't want to be stagnant. I want to spend my life letting the Living Water of God flow from and through me.

If you are feeling stagnant today, check your connection to the Fountain of Living Water. Then turn on the spigot of your heart and let God's love flow—let the blessings and the truth and the love out where it can bless others.

Life is in the flowing water.

Dear Jesus, You gave Your life so that I could have Living Water in my soul. Water that joyously bubbles life and liberty. Help me to faithfully share Your Living Water with the thirsty people around me.

Don't let me become stagnant, hoarding Your blessings in my heart. I give myself to Your service. Strengthen me to be faithful. In Your precious name I pray.

Think About It:
- Are you feeling stagnant?
- Are you connected to the Source of Living Water, which is Jesus the Christ?
- How can you share the blessings of Living Water with others?

Grace When Malware Strikes

*Be sober, be vigilant; because your adversary the devil, as
a roaring lion, walketh about, seeking whom he may devour:*
—1 Peter 5:8

Recently, I spent 45 minutes uninstalling a variety of programs that were installed when I inadvertently clicked a link while doing research. I thought I'd declined the programs, but somehow they managed to install. I will admit user error is a possibility, but I will also state that the installation protocol was deceptive. I know you might be shocked.

While uninstalling the reprobate programs, I noticed several other apps that had crept onto my hard drive unawares. I wonder if these programs were the ones causing my computer to slow down and act strangely. Regardless, they sat there eating up memory and energy, and I was clueless about their existence until I began reviewing the list. They, too, bit the dust during my cleanup.

I consider myself a cautious web user. I maintain an updated anti-virus program that scans regularly, so this was surprising to me. How did these things sneak in?

I'm not sure about the unwanted computer programs, but I know that reprobate programs sometimes sneak into my heart as well.

I let my guard down, and the intentions and attitudes of the world attach themselves to my heart and begin to take control. I adopt negative feelings and judgmental opinions. My joy begins to sputter, my focus turns inward, and my spiritual life slows down. I find myself reacting in ways that I know are not right.

I wonder how those mindsets take over. How do they take over so quickly? But unfortunately, I know how it happens.

I have an enemy—an enemy that is worse than any malware that has ever troubled my computer. The Bible compares him to a roaring lion roaming about to see "whom he can devour" (1 Peter 5:8). When I let down my guard, when I focus on the world rather than God's Word, when my eyes are on me rather than on Jesus, I become vulnerable to his attack. He is vigilant when I am not.

This could make me run scared, but I know something (make that Someone) who can clean up my heart and my mind. He offers me the power to be victorious in the face of this enemy, and He has promised never to leave me.

That enemy continues to roam and look to make me his next meal, wishing to scramble my thoughts and feelings like eggs in a frying pan, but greater is He (Jesus) that is in me than he (Satan) that is in the world.

Victory requires dependence on God's Word and vigilance, which looks a lot like obedience to God, to stop the enemy in his tracks. I am so thankful that God has given me His Spirit to defrag my thoughts and help me spot the enemy's programs. I am so thankful that when my heart drive is in disarray, He is willing and able to clean me up and allow me to be useful to Him.

Just like I need to check my computer hard drive regularly, I need to ask the Holy Spirit to check my heart drive. He alone can strengthen me to stand and remain faithful in a world filled with Satan's malware.

Father, You warned me about the maliciousness of the enemy, but You also have promised to be with me as I stand against him. Keep me vigilant, Father. Let me not take for granted the armor that You have provided, so that I may stand in the evil days that surround us. I know that You are my King. Search me and know my heart. See if there is any wicked way in me. In Jesus' name.

Think About It:
- Have you asked God to check your heart drive lately?
- Psalm 139:23-24 is a good place to start.
- 1 John 1:9 is a great follow-up verse.

What's in a Name?

But now thus saith the Lord that created thee, O Jacob, and he that formed thee, O Israel, Fear not: for I have redeemed thee, I have called thee by thy name; thou art mine.
—Isaiah 43:1

Ask any substitute teacher—names are powerful tools. Students behave differently when they believe they are anonymous. Call one by name, and suddenly, the atmosphere changes.

And I beg to differ with Shakespeare's statement, "What's in a name? That which we call a rose by any other name would smell as sweet."[5] While technically true, we all know that names can color our perceptions.

Names are powerful.

Parents recognize this when a baby is on the way. They search for just the right name. Sometimes they want the name to convey heritage, so they choose an honored loved one's name. Sometimes they research the meanings of names and choose one that has the characteristic they hope to instill in their child. Other times, they choose a name because of its sound or beauty. Whatever the name, it goes with the child from birth to the grave, and it becomes a symbol of who he is and how he is recognized.

Names go beyond those given at birth, however. Humans have a way of assigning names based on their perception of actions, character, or looks. So, we end up with titles like stupid, clumsy, fat, idiot, crazy, dull, and ugly. These names pass judgment, and they move from the surface to the soul to wound and scar. Sometimes these titles take prominence over the carefully chosen names of birth, and too often they become the way we think of ourselves, and we find ourselves calling ourselves by these names.

God understands the importance of names. Reading through the Bible is always an adventure as we attempt to pronounce unfamiliar names, but those names carried meaning for their bearers. Adam – the man; Eve – living; Joshua – one who saves; Judah – praise; Sarah – princess; Abraham – multitude of nations; Peter – rock; Immanuel – God with us. These are just a few of the descriptive names God used for His people. Name is so important to God, that one of the Ten Commandments warns us against taking His name in vain (using it lightly or carelessly).

God's understanding of the power of a name goes well beyond the name given at birth or rebirth, and He, too, uses names that describe. Throughout scripture, He calls His children by names that reassure and empower them. These names help us stand against the world's onslaught. They describe our relationship to Him, and they connect us to His heart.

Here are a few of God's names for His children:
- chosen – 1 Peter 2:9
- new creation – 2 Corinthians 5:17
- redeemed – Psalm 107:2
- holy – 1 Peter 1:15
- righteous – 1 Peter 3:12
- overcomer – 1 John 5:4
- friend – John 15:15
- His child – Galatians 3:26
- royalty – 1 Peter 2:9
- warrior or soldier – 2 Timothy 2:4

This world has a way of tearing down, and the enemy labels God's children in ways that hurt and destroy. God, however, lifts His children up, calling us to see ourselves as He sees us. This amazes me.

You may be sitting in your natty robe with unbrushed teeth nursing a cup of coffee, but God sees His creation—His loved child. When we come to Him in trust, He makes us new, imparting His goodness and grace into our souls. So, see yourself as God sees you. Let the power of His names for you fortify your soul in a world of sarcasm and negativity.

Father, I am amazed that You have called me Your own child, precious in Your sight. You call me holy, saint, though I struggle to see myself in that light. Thank You for giving me Your name, for making me a member of Your family. I praise You for calling me Your own. Let me live as Yours.

Think About It:
- What name would you give yourself?
- Do you see yourself as God sees you?
- How can you learn to see yourself as God sees you?

Trophy of Grace

As day fades into evening,
my weary mind seeks rest.
I pull aside to listen to
the One Who knows me best.

He quietly brings to my heart
His words of gentle grace.
He calls me from my worry
into His holy place.

He tells me of my destiny;
He calls me His redeemed.
His grace sings over me with love
and heals my frazzled dreams.

I never want to pull away
from His holy place,
yet He sends me out renewed—
a trophy of His grace.

Grace to Be a Barnabas

*I have shown you all things, how that so laboring ye ought
to support the weak, and to remember the words of the Lord Jesus,
how he said, It is more blessed to give than to receive.*
—Acts 20:35

Can you imagine going nose-to-nose with the Apostle Paul, challenging a decision he made? I can't.

But Barnabas did.

Barnabas, whose name means *son of encouragement,* had been with Paul from the beginning of Paul's ministry. He was the one who introduced Paul to the other apostles after Paul's conversion. Barnabas vouched for Paul's faith and the change that had occurred because of his encounter with Christ.

"But Barnabas took him (Paul), and brought him to the apostles, and declared unto them how he had seen the Lord in the way, and that he had spoken to him, and how he had preached boldly at Damascus in the name of Jesus" (Acts 9:27).

Barnabas stuck his neck out and linked his reputation to the reputation of Paul. (Remember that the apostles still saw Paul as the one who had sought out and killed Christians.)

In the New Testament, Barnabas is most frequently mentioned in the book of Acts, where his name appears in 27 verses. He also appears in Paul's letters in 1 Corinthians 9:6, Galatians 2:1, 2:9, 2:13, and Colossians 4:10. His name is usually found joined to Paul's, and always, he is found supporting and encouraging believers. When revival broke out in Antioch and Gentiles were coming to Christ, the church in Jerusalem sent Barnabas to check things out. He not only verified the teaching, but he also joined in (Acts 11:23).

Barnabas was a good man, and he was a bold witness for Jesus. He travelled with Paul on his first missionary journey after being anointed by the apostles. He was referred to as a prophet and teacher (Acts 13:1). He was with Paul when Paul spoke to the Grecians and when He was stoned in Acts 14.

My favorite story about Barnabas, though, involves a disagreement he had with Paul in the fifteenth chapter of Acts. On an earlier journey, they had taken a young man by the name of John Mark with them. Sometime during the trip, John Mark left and went home. This evidently did not sit well with Paul.

Later, Paul and Barnabas prepared to go back and encourage the new believers that had come to the Lord. Barnabas wanted to take John Mark with them again. This is what happened: "But Paul thought not good to take him (John Mark) with them, who departed from them from Pamphylia, and went not with them to the work. And the contention was so sharp between them, that they departed asunder one from the other: and so Barnabas took Mark, and sailed unto Cyprus; And Paul chose Silas, and departed, being recommended by the brethren unto the grace of God" (Acts 15:38–40).

Why is this my favorite story? Here I see the heart of Barnabas. He was not willing to give up on John Mark because of his earlier failure. He believed that John Mark was worth taking another chance on. So much so that he stood up to Paul regarding Paul's dismissal of Mark. He then made John Mark his partner in evangelism in lieu of Paul.

This John Mark that Barnabas stuck his neck out for was the Mark who wrote the second gospel of the New Testament. While we read only two passing references to Barnabas after Acts 15, Paul later referred to Mark's active service, "Only Luke is with me. Take Mark, and bring him with thee: for he is profitable to me for the ministry" (2 Timothy 4:11).

Mark, who had failed, was now a profitable minister. Why? I believe that Mark's growth in the Lord was largely due to the encouragement and teaching of Barnabas.

Son of Encouragement describes Barnabas' ministry. He took the immature and the untested and he nurtured them along in faith. He set an example for me.

I can choose to encourage rather than condemn. I can choose to lift up rather than criticize. (After all, God has not appointed me to be the quality control manager of the world.) I can choose to support and teach rather than dismiss those around me.

I can choose to be a Barnabas.

Father, sometimes it is easy to overlook those who are young or struggling, but you have called me to lift up and encourage. Help me to notice and to purposefully reach out to those around me who need an encouraging word or a helping hand. Lead me to those that you would have me mentor and help me to faithfully follow you in this task. Show me the one who needs another chance. Push me out of my comfort zone, Lord, into your zone of service. Help me to follow the example that Jesus set and that Barnabas followed. In Jesus's name I pray.

Think About It:
- How can you be an encourager to those around you?
- Is there someone you are called to mentor?

Grace When We Are Wilting

Now unto him that is able to keep you from falling, and to present you faultless before the presence of his glory with exceeding joy,
—Jude 24

"Chrysanthemum wilted." This is my very favorite line from the children's book, *Chrysanthemum*, by Kevin Henkes.[7]

In the story, Chrysanthemum begins school, believing in the beauty of her name, only to have her spirit crushed by the teasing of the other children. "Chrysanthemum wilted" describes her response.

I can see this and feel this, because there have been days and times that I have wilted, too. Times when enduring ongoing conflict seemed more than I could bear. Times when the day's demands outlasted my energy. Times when my motives were questioned, and my character was challenged. Times when hopelessness outweighed hope and darkness threatened to shut out the light.

Dry times. Hard times. Discouraging times. Like Chrysanthemum, I wilted.

Wilting is not a pleasant experience. It brings to mind the flower, thirsty for water, that droops over the side of the pot. If it doesn't get water soon, it will not survive.

What can we do to prevent and survive wilting? God has some resources for us.

1. Meditate (think) on God's Word.

We think about a lot of things during each day. Instead of providing strength, many of our thoughts bring drought to our souls. In the story about Chrysanthemum, she wilted because she was listening to the wrong voices. We can trust what God has to say. His Word sustains and enriches.

"But his delight is in the law of the Lord; and in His law doth he meditate day and night. And he shall be like a tree planted by the rivers of water, that bringeth forth his fruit in his season; his leaf also shall not wither; and whatsoever he doeth shall prosper" (Psalm 1:2-3).

God's Word has the power to strengthen our souls and to prepare us for times when wilting might occur. It is a powerful resource for us.

2. Commit your way to God.

There are many things in this life that I do not understand, but I know that God has a plan for me. He will provide what I need as I follow Him.

"I have set the Lord always before me: because he is at my right hand, I shall not be moved. Therefore my heart is glad, and my glory rejoices: my flesh also shall rest in hope" (Psalm 16:8-9).

"It is God that girds me with strength, and makes my way perfect" (Psalm 18:32).

3. Wait for God's timing.

We are impatient creatures who want what we want when we want it, so we wilt because we become weary in the waiting. God calls us to trust the timetable to Him, knowing that He desires the best for us.

"I had fainted, unless I had believed to see the goodness of the Lord in the land of the living.

Wait on the Lord: be of good courage, and He shall strengthen your heart: wait, I say, on the Lord" (Psalm 27:13-14).

4. Practice Praise.

Praise lifts us above our circumstances into the presence of God. When we choose to praise, we are choosing to trust His way. We are looking beyond what our eyes can see to where faith calls us.

"I will bless the Lord at all times: His praise shall continually be in my mouth" (Psalm 34:1).

"Be glad in the Lord, and rejoice, ye righteous: and shout for joy, all ye that are upright in heart" (Psalm 32:11).

5. Focus on the good.

There are many things in this life to catch our attention. Where we choose to focus will help determine how inclined we are to wilt. We are in charge of our thoughts, and we can choose to look for the good and the right in each day.

"Finally, brethren, whatsoever things are true, whatsoever things are honest, whatsoever things are just, whatsoever things are pure, whatsoever things are lovely, whatsoever things are of good report; if there be any virtue, and if there be any praise, think on these things" (Philippians 4:8).

If you are feeling a bit wilted today, open God's word, and spend some time there. The verses in this post are just a miniscule sampling of the riches you will find. Commit your life and your way to God. Wait for Him to answer your prayers and praise Him as you wait. Check out where your thoughts are. What is something good or beautiful you saw today? Think on these things.

Father, we are prone to wilt in this dry world. Too often we let our hearts get too far from Your Living Water. Today, I want to focus my heart on the goodness of who You are and the promises of Your word. Today, I want to look for the blessings in life and praise You for all that You are doing. Today, I once again commit my life, my whole life to Your plan, to wait patiently for You to complete Your work in me. Revive my heart, Lord. You do good work. Please do it in me.

Think About It:
- Do you feel like you are wilting today?
- What are some steps that you can take to recover from wilt?
- What will you do to prevent wilt in your life?

Send Down the Rain

Parched by the heat of the journey,
broken and cracked by the intense demands of the day,
my soul thirsts for refreshment—
clear waters washing over my weary feet,
drops of spring rain scattering dust as they fall.
I am dry, Lord.
Send down Your rain—
the cleansing water of Your word
to wash my dusty soul,
the invigorating showers of blessing
to fill the empty cisterns of my heart.
I am dry, Lord.
Send down Your rain—
grow my roots deep,
cause my leaves to flourish
bearing fruit in abundance.
Let me dance in the raindrops of Your love—
Lord, send down Your rain.

Grace for Everyday Cleaning

Wash me and I shall be whiter than snow… Create in me a clean heart, O God: and renew a right spirit within me.
—Psalms 51:7, 10

Carpets cleaned—check.
Tile sanitized—check.
Draperies laundered—check.
Humans enter—oh well.

Spring cleaning tasks are necessary. They go beyond the routine vacuuming and dusting and reach into the crevices where month-old crumbs lie hidden and the detritus from the last popcorn-and-movie night has turned green.

Enter broom, mop, steamer, and a hefty dose of cleanser; work begins. Hard, exhausting, back-breaking work that moves furniture and climbs to reach ceiling fans long forgotten.

At the end of the day (or week), satisfaction blooms as the clean kingdom is reviewed and relished.

But it doesn't last.

People are messy, even when they don't mean to be. Dirt accumulates, pet hair swirls, and the tracks where someone forgot to remove shoes—yep, they are splayed across the floor like sprinkles on a birthday cake.

Routines exist that keep cleaning up to date and less onerous, but we don't always follow those routines. Just one day or three days or a week without sweeping won't matter, will it? We have so many other things that we must (want to) do.

Sort of reminds us of how we treat sin in our lives, doesn't it?

The Israelites in the Old Testament are prime examples of how human nature works. Just read through the books of history in Judges, Samuel, Kings, and Chronicles. Over and over the cycle repeats.

A good king or a judge would call the people to task, and they would destroy the idols, break down the high places where sacrifices to idols were offered, and turn back to God. They would enjoy the blessing of close relationship with Him, but gradually sin would creep back in. The idols would be reinstated, and the hearts of the people would turn away from the God Who chose them and redeemed them.

A verse regarding King Rehoboam in 2 Chronicles 13 sums it up, "And he did evil, because he prepared not his heart to seek the Lord" (2 Chronicles 13:14).

Rehoboam was Solomon's son. He knew the right way; he just decided his way was better.

It is easy to look at the history of Israel, shake our heads, and say "Why couldn't they learn?". I mean God was working with them. He had parted the sea and performed miracles untold for this recalcitrant people. What gives? Why couldn't they get it right?

I ask myself the same question sometimes.

God has redeemed me, purchased me with the blood of His own Son, provided for me, kept me, and yet...

Rather than dealing with sin through confession and repentance daily, I let it build up in my heart—grudges, self-sufficiency, unkind thoughts, lack of love. I offer God a dead sacrifice from the past instead of the living sacrifice of everyday worship and service (Romans 12:1-2). Don't kid yourself—dead smells.

I can wait for some big happening or church service to rededicate my life (spring cleaning of the soul), and don't get me wrong, repentance and confession are always important, or I can daily submit my life, my desires, my tasks, my vision, my future, my walk to His loving control. You know, a "living sacrifice". I can refuse to allow sin to take up residence or be comfortable in my heart. God has even provided a way for routine cleaning that allows me to enjoy an open and joyous relationship with Him.

"If we confess our sins, He is faithful and just to forgive us our sins, and to cleanse us from all unrighteousness" (1 John 1:9).

God has made a way; Jesus paid the price. Am I willing to follow His steps?

I think today is a good day to do a sweep of my heart and see if there is anything there that needs to be cleaned out.

Gracious Father, You are more than I could ever desire. You are my heart, my life, my destiny. I offer all of me to all of You today. Please sweep any cobwebs from my heart and let it be completely clean for You. I love You, Lord. In Jesus' precious name I pray.

Think About It:
- When was the last time you took a spiritual inventory of your heart?
- Is today a day when some cleaning is needed?

Send Down the Hail

Thou therefore, my son, be strong in the grace that is in Christ Jesus.
—2 Timothy 2:2

The battle was on.

The kings had heard of Joshua's victory of Ai and of his treaty with Gibeon, and they were worried. They saw Gibeon as a formidable foe by itself. Now joined with the army of Israel, nothing would stop them.

So, five kings with their armies joined together as a force to attack Gibeon. The men of Gibeon called in a favor from Joshua for his support in the battle. Joshua stood true to his word and went to help Gibeon. There would be a battle, but God had assured Joshua of victory.

"And the Lord said unto Joshua, Fear them not: for I have delivered them into thine hand; there shall not a man of them stand before thee" (Joshua 10:8).

Several miracles occurred during this battle. Joshua prayed, and God caused the sun to stand still, and, later, God sent hail to batter the armies of the five kings as they ran from the battle.

"And it came to pass, as they fled from before Israel, and were in the going down to Bethhoron, that the Lord cast down great stones from heaven upon them unto Azekah, and they died: they were more which died with hailstones than they whom the children of Israel slew with the sword" (Joshua 10:11).

I want to talk about that hail.

Couldn't God have just skipped the battle and sent down the hail to begin with? God gave Joshua assurance of victory, but He never released him from the call to fight. Couldn't He have conquered the land without calling His people into battle?

The battle is on in my life every day.

I often pray for God to send down the hail when He is calling me into battle. I want Him to just fix the problems, but He wants me to engage with and obey His word.
- He calls me to be persistent in prayer.
- He calls me to stand when it seems that everything is wrong.
- He calls me to have courage when I am afraid.
- He calls me to get involved with people when I am not sure how to help.
- He calls me to speak up when I see injustice.
- He calls me to serve when the duty is hard.
- He calls me to have hope when all around is hopeless.
- He calls me to speak grace into suffering.
- He calls me to show up every day to do the right thing.

My heart does not relish the battle or the suffering. My spirit grows weary in waiting and loses courage in the face of evil, and I wonder why He doesn't just send down the hail to wipe out the enemy.

God does intervene, and miracles occur, but He never releases me from the battle. In fact, He reminds me to be a good soldier and to fully clothe myself in His armor (Ephesians 6:10-18).

As long as I live, there will be battles to fight:
- over pride
- over self-centeredness
- over greed
- over hatred
- over lies
- over apathy
- over self-indulgence
- over injustice
- over unbelief
- over hurt and pain and grief

God has called me just as He called Joshua to "be strong and very courageous" (Joshua 1:7), knowing that He goes before me and with me into every battle. There is no quitting in His army. He has promised victory, and when the time is right, He will send down the hail.

Father, I confess that I don't like the battles. I get tired of fighting against my flesh and against the evil in this world. Help me, though, to be a good soldier for You, to not entangle myself with the cares of this life, to lean wholly on Your word, Your truth, knowing that when the time is right You will send down the hail.

Think About It:
- When is it hardest for you to stand firm for Christ?
- What battles are you facing now?
- What scriptures can help you as you face these battles?

Grace to do the Right Things

I will praise thee, O Lord, with my whole heart; I will shew forth all thy marvelous works. I will be glad and rejoice in thee: I will sing praise to thy name, O thou most High... But the Lord shall endure for ever: he hath prepared his throne for judgment. And he shall judge the world in righteousness, he shall minister judgment to the people in uprightness.
—Psalm 9:1-2, 7-8

This Life!

Every day we deal with and live in the skirmishes of the evil one, but God knows this battle has been fought and is completed. It was fought at the cross and finished in the resurrection.

The evil one still grapples for a foothold in the lives of humans causing havoc and grief, but his days are numbered.

Even before the cross, God's people knew that the ultimate victory belongs to God, not Satan. David knew this. Daily, he maneuvered through the madness of Saul and the treacheries and treason in the nation of Israel, but his hope, his foundation, his trust was in God. Psalm nine is one of the psalms in which David proclaims God's victory as a feat accomplished (Psalm 9:5–8, 15–20).

We can learn from David's response to the physical and spiritual battles he faced. Four actions described in this psalm give us guidance for our daily lives in this world.

What did David do?

- **He sang praises to God** (verse 11). When the darkness seemed overwhelming, David used his eyes of faith to look beyond the immediate to the eternal. This vision filled his heart with song.

- **He declared God's work** (verse 11). In our world, much time and energy is spent proclaiming the enemy's work – just listen to the daily news. Conversations center around the bad and the ugly, and the good lies ignored by the wayside. David, though, talked about God's work.
- **He cried for God's mercy** as he lived through troubled times (verse 13). Make no mistake, we need God's mercy in this world. We cannot live victorious lives in our own strength. David knew this and cried for God to have mercy on him.
- **He rejoiced in God's salvation** (verse 14). This world is not my home. I have been redeemed by the precious blood of Jesus Christ. No matter what is happening or not happening, I can rejoice that I am His child. He is my refuge (verse 9). He has not forsaken, and He will not forsake me (verse 10).

David's response to this troubled world did not come from a life free of trial. It flowed from a heart of faith in the everlasting God.

I have often heard that success comes when we do the right things over and over again. David gives us, through God's inspiration, the right things to do.

In this broken world, do your trials seem overwhelming? Does it appear that evil is winning?

Then, do the right things:
- Sing praises to God.
- Tell others about Him and His work.
- Cry out for His mercy.
- Rejoice in His salvation

Whether it feels reasonable or not, keep doing the right things—every. day.

Victory is certain. God has promised, and we know He always keeps His promises. We can live in God's victory rather than the evil one's despair.

Father, Some days life is hard, and doing the right thing is even harder. Give me the strength and the faith to keep doing the right things every day knowing that You are the victor. You are King. I can rejoice in Your salvation. As I do the right things, You can work Your will through me, because You keep Your word. Help me to be faithful, Lord, as You are faithful.

Think About It:
- Which of these things is the hardest for you to do when you are going through a trial?
- Which is the easiest?

Passion

Yea doubtless, and I count all things but loss for the excellency of the knowledge of Christ Jesus my Lord: for whom I have suffered the loss of all things, and do count them but dung, that I may win Christ, And be found in him, not having mine own righteousness, which is of the law, but that which is through the faith of Christ, the righteousness which is of God by faith: That I may know him, and the power of his resurrection, and the fellowship of his sufferings, being made conformable unto his death;
—Philippians 3:8–10

Talk to my husband for more than five minutes and he is going to whip out his phone and begin showing you pictures of the grandchildren or children or places he has visited. He is passionate about many things, and he loves to share his passions with others.

If cell phones had been available in the first century, I believe that the Apostle Paul would have waylaid everyone he met to show them a picture of Jesus. He didn't have a cell phone, so God allowed him to use words instead. Paul's passion revealed itself in the words he wrote, and it is evident that his passion was Jesus the Christ.

Merriam-Webster gives one definition of passion as an "intense, driving, or overmastering feeling or conviction."[6]

This definition is fully displayed in Paul's life. He pressed on. Persecution didn't stop him. Deprivation didn't stop him. Weariness didn't stop him. He continued. Why? Because of his love, his passion, for Jesus Christ. He served, not out of duty, but out of gratitude for Christ's work in his life.

I hear Paul's passion in the words to the Corinthian church, "And I, brethren, when I came to you, came not with excellency of speech or of wisdom, declaring unto you the testimony of God. For I determined not to know any thing among you, save Jesus Christ, and him crucified" (1 Corinthians 2:1–2).

While I am sure of Paul's conviction, I wonder about my own passion for Jesus. As I flip through the photos in my brain, how many of them are of Him?

I can be passionate about a cause, passionate about service, passionate about holy living or Bible study or a talent or gift, but unless these passions stem from my love for Jesus Christ, they are futile. Only as my heart seeks Him, abides in Him, will my life bear fruit that honors Him.

Service that devolves into duty and passionate task completion are not good enough. He calls me to His heart. He calls me to love Him.

Today, I am checking my heart and reviewing its photo album. I want Jesus to be the star that shines there.

An old quote from Dr. Curtis Hutson, who pastored in Georgia during the sixties and seventies, goes like this, "I want to love Him so much that when I look up and say, 'Jesus, I love You', He'll look down and say, 'I know.'"

That is my goal today. How about you?

Father, stir my heart with love for You today. Let there be no doubt Who is center stage in my heart.

Think About It:
- Where do most of your thoughts center throughout the day?
- What or whom are you passionate about?
- How can you be more passionate about Jesus?

I Want to Love Him So Much

I want to love Him so much
That when I look up and say
Jesus, I love You,
He'll look down and say I know.

Words are so easily spoken
Promises made and then broken
Daily life leads in to sin and defeat.
Trials come, I fall
Although I want most of all
To lay a crown at my Savior's feet.

I want each step that I take
And each decision I make
To bring honor to my Savior's name.
I need His strength each day
To follow in His way.
To live for Jesus is my highest aim.

He proved His love for me
When there on Calvary
He stretched out his arms and died so willingly.
Now every day in every way
I want my life to say
Thank You for all You've done for me.

Words of Grace

In the multitude of words sin is not lacking, But he who restrains his lips is wise.
—Proverbs 10:19

When a jar of pickled peppers falls off the refrigerator shelf onto a tile floor, it makes a big mess. I know this, because a recent morning found me on my hands and knees cleaning up peppers, sticky syrup and broken glass.

It was a small jar, but the mess created was worthy of a gallon bucket.

I should probably say here that I am known in my household for placing jars too close to the edge in the refrigerator, fitting one more thing on a shelf, thinking I will find a better place for that later.

That morning later happened.

The thing about a jar crashing onto the floor is that the damage is ongoing. I can clean up the immediate mess, place everything in the garbage, wash out the cleaning cloths and think, "Done!" but it isn't done. Little pieces of glass find their way into the oddest corners. I will come across them eventually, sometimes with a broom, sometimes with a foot. Managing to find and pick up every little piece at the time of the accident just doesn't happen.

On that morning, God reminded me, while I was on my knees cleaning, that my words and actions are just like that.

I can vent my frustration toward something or someone, and I can apologize, but little shards of hurt are hard to collect from the heart. I can thoughtlessly put my own feelings and needs first in a situation and make a big mess. The little pieces of remembrance that stick in the other person's soul may hide from my regret for days or weeks or years.

There is always shrapnel from an explosion. Shrapnel is hard to clean up, and the wounds are difficult to mend.

Reminder to myself - prevention is better than clean up. Put the jars at the back of the refrigerator shelf!

Guard my actions and words toward others.

Pickled peppers and unkindness are both horrendous to clean up.

"Let your speech be always with grace" (Colossians 4:6).

Father, guard my words today. I don't want them to spill out on someone like those pickled peppers spilled out all over the floor. I don't want to be trying to clean up the shrapnel from someone's heart that I have put there. Let your Holy Spirit guide my lips to speak words that encourage and edify, words that strengthen and lead others to love You. Thank You for giving me the right words to say. I love You, Lord.

Think About It:
- Has there ever been a time when your words were like those pickled peppers and you wished you could take them all back?
- How did you handle the situation?
- How can you ask God to help you control your tongue in the future?

Shine On

Across the sky, spangled stars
move in their steady course.
Uniquely shaped,
uniquely placed
for one task—
to light the night.

Across the world, redeemed people
move through their daily lives.
Uniquely shaped,
uniquely placed
for one task—
to light the world.

Grace to Rejoice Always

Yet I will rejoice in the Lord, I will joy in the God of my salvation.
—Habakkuk 3:18

A while back, after a particularly trying day and a particularly trying encounter with a particularly angry person, I made a commitment to myself—I choose joy, no matter what.

I was putting up my umbrella of joy, and no one or no thing was going to rain on my parade!

That is scriptural, right? After all, "the joy of the Lord is your strength" (Nehemiah 8:10), and Paul says to "rejoice always" (1 Thessalonians 5:16).

Those were my thoughts, so I drew my line in the sand. While I would care and pray and serve, I would not allow the grumps and groans of each day or each person to drag me down. I would not!

Within two days a hurricane destroyed my umbrella, and the thunderstorms did not stop.

The litany of occurrences and mishaps over the next few weeks are not important. What is important to note is that I decided, and the trials of life immediately began to test that commitment.

Every. Day.

So, what am I to learn from this?

The first realization I made was that there was a whole lot of "I" in my commitment. "I choose, I put up, my parade, I drew, I would not..." You get the picture. My commitment depended on and was centered in me. My joy.

The joy of the Lord exists in the middle of trials and problems. If joy is a river, it flows from the fountain of Living Water—Jesus Christ. It supersedes circumstances because it is centered in the Lord. It lives in my reliance on and trust in Him. The joy of the Lord lives in my

Lord, and I access it as I depend wholly on Him, no matter what is going around me. Joy is a fruit of the Holy Spirit working in my life (Galatians 5:22). It is not a line in the sand; it is a living relationship with my Lord.

Can it sustain me in times of difficulty and trial? Absolutely! But it won't be because I stiffened my backbone and determined it so. It will be because I carried every care to my Father.

The second realization is that there will always be trial. As long as I am in this world, I will deal with fallen, imperfect people (one of which is me) and circumstances skewed by the prince of this world. I cannot isolate myself from frustrations and annoyances and aggravations and sorrow; they are the currency of doing business in this world.

Jesus promised there would be trouble in this life, but He also promised His peace (John 16:33) and His joy (John 15:11). I must cling closely to Him. He is the One with authority and power over evil.

My third realization was the reminder that Jesus is my very present help. I may be wading through the swamp, but He holds me up. He gives me strength. He will see me through.

Even though my umbrella was demolished, God's joy still resounds in my heart. Some days it happily crashes and tumbles like a rushing stream, and other days it flows quietly, soothing my heart. The joy of the Lord is unstoppable, unquenchable, and not dependent on my lines in the sand.

That is why I can rejoice always.

Father, happiness in this world is such a fragile thing, but Your joy is durable, sustaining me through the toughest of trials. When I become frustrated, help me to remember to lean into You, for there I will find renewed peace for my journey. This life is so temporary. Remind me to "count it all joy" as I walk with You.

Think About It:
- What events have the most effect on your joy?
- When was a time that Christ helped you through a trying time with joy?
- Why is joy so important?

Always With Me

Thou wilt keep him in perfect peace, whose mind is stayed on thee: because he trusts in thee.
—Isaiah 26:3

Quiet. Stillness. Peace.

When I read the Psalms, I often picture David in the quiet of the field, close to his sheep, basking in the quiet and the presence of God. He strums his harp and sings to God. Tranquility and peace reign. This is probably not an accurate picture, but I like it.

I love times of quiet aloneness with God, times of separation from the panicked pace of this world. These times feed my soul.

But that is not everyday life for me, and David did not live apart from confusion and trial either.

Many of the Psalms were written, not from a shepherd's field, but from caves. He wrote during wilderness wanderings as he ran from the treacheries of Saul. He wrote in times of desperate despair and after times of great sin. He wrote when his soul was full of questions.

David's life was not one of peace and tranquility. He was threatened and falsely accused, chased and hounded, burdened with the leadership of a fledgling nation, charged with protection against enemy armies, tempted and sorely tried. His family was a mess, and he suffered great sorrow.

Yet, still the Psalms, those songs of praise and prayers of petition, came. Still, David looked to the God of his heart for rescue, comfort, forgiveness, and grace. Still, he faithfully offered praise to God.

Here is the truth.

God is with me whether I am sitting in my favorite chair with my special cup of coffee, reading my Bible, or frantically fighting against the evil in this world. His presence surrounds me in trial and in triumph. He walks with me in the middle of every mess in my life. I do not have to be in a particular place or a tidy situation to experience His amazing peace.

That is why I can say with David, "Yea, though I walk through the valley of the shadow of death, I will fear no evil: for Thou art with me; thy rod and thy staff comfort me" (Psalm 23:4).

While I long to pull away from the world and its problems, God often places me squarely in the heart of difficulty, and there He shows me that He is God and He can carry me through.

God's light shines in my darkness and His love holds me in the storm.

I am not perfect, and my life is not flawless, but I serve a perfect God. When I struggle, this is the truth I must remember and the certainty to which I must cling, no matter where I am.

Father, thank You for Your constant presence and Your promise to always be with me. Thank You for shining Your light in my darkness. Help me to cling to the certainty of Your word and Your faithfulness with all my being no matter what circumstances surround me. I praise You. I love You. You are my Comfort, my Rock, and my Fortress, the One that I trust. In Jesus' name I pray.

Think About It:
- Where is your favorite place to seek God?
- In what ways do you find it hard to pray when difficulties arise in your life?
- How has God helped you in times of trial?

Grace to Make the Best Choices

But I will sing of Thy power; yea, I will sing aloud of Thy mercy in the morning: for Thou has been my defense and refuge in the day of my trouble. Unto Thee, O my strength, will I sing: for God is my defense, and the God of my mercy.
—Psalm 59:16–17

Troubled, evil, raging, distraught, and crumbling are all words that come to mind when I think about the happenings in our world today. With Dorothy, I have to say "Toto, we are not in Kansas anymore."[8]

But is this the first time the world has gone awry?

I hear people longing for the 'good old days', and I admit that I sometimes join them, but has there been a time since Eve succumbed to the slippery words of the serpent that evil has not been rearing its ugly head? It may be less restrained today. It may be closer to me and invading my comfort zone now, but evil has always been on the warpath against good, against right, against TRUTH, against GOD.

In Psalm 59, around three thousand years ago, David railed against the evil attacking his world. His descriptions are amazingly like the occurrences in our nation and world today. Check it out:

- They lie in wait for my soul. (verse 3)
- The powerful are gathered against the righteous. (verse 3)
- They prowl in the dark. (verse 6)
- Filth comes from their mouths. (verse 7)
- Their words cut. (verse 7)
- They think no one can detect their deviousness. (verse 7)
- They are filled with cursing and lying. (verse 12)
- They are filled with pride. (verse 12)

Pick your "they" in today's news, and you will find that the descriptions above apply.

How do we respond as Christians? In the conflict and the danger that surrounded, how did David respond three thousand years ago? We can read his responses in Psalm 59.

- **David cried to God for help and deliverance** (verses 1, 4-5, 11-13). He didn't just cry one time; he cried repeatedly. David knew that only God could provide the wisdom that he needed to survive. Only God could deliver him.
- **David waited on (depended on) God** (verses 9-10). David had times in his life that he acted rashly and outside of God's will for him, but when he waited on God, the right answer always came.
- **He determined to sing of God's power, God's mercy, God's defense and refuge** (verses 16-17). David refused to be silent about his God. He refused to be intimidated by the enemy that wanted to silence God's song. David made up his mind to sing of God. The act of determining or choosing is a strong act that God can use. Before the challenge, before entering the war, David decided to sing.

I like David's choices.

This morning, though dark clouds may gather, though trouble may loom on the horizon and the future may seem unsure:

- I will commit my way and the world to the mercy of God. I will cry for His mercy.
- I will depend on Him for guidance and deliverance.
- I will praise His unfailing love and sing of His power and His mercy.
- I will stand in His TRUTH.

I will not despair, and I will not be silent, for He is the God of my mercy, and He has been and will be my "refuge in the day of my trouble" (Psalm 59:16).

See those "I wills" and "I will nots"? Those are choices.

God help me make the right ones—Every. Day.

Father, my choices have not always been right, but I want them to be. I want to stand for You each day. I want to depend on You and praise You even when storm clouds gather. I want to sing of Your love and mercy in the face of the evil in this world. Grant strength to make it so, Lord. You are the God of my mercy, and You are my refuge every day of my life. I stand in the truth of who You are.

Think About It:
- What choices are you making today?
- How will those choices affect how you live today?
- How will they affect those around you?

God in His Grace Provides

But godliness with contentment is great gain.
—1 Timothy 6:6

Blessed beyond measure! That was the status of the Israelites as they wandered in the wilderness.

They walked for miles and for years, but their shoes never wore out. Their food rained down from Heaven each day. When they needed water, God provided that, too.

Think of waking up every morning, walking out on your lawn, and picking up breakfast. No trips to your favorite stores. No wandering through the aisles trying to find the right brand. No checkout lines to wait in. That would even beat ordering your groceries online. God always goes beyond what is necessary to show His love, so I know that the manna tasted good, too.

The Israelites, though, got a little tired of it. You know, fried manna for breakfast, manna sandwiches for lunch, and manna meatloaf with mashed manna for dinner. They had plenty—over and above what they needed—but they were not satisfied. They wanted something different, so they complained.

Their attitude sort of reminds me of myself. Sometimes I think, "Lord, I could sure use a little of that manna. Could you drop some down?" I look at the vehicle in the garage, still running well, and say, "A new car sure would smell nice", or I walk through my comfortable home and determine, "gotta have a new rug." I may even bite into a chicken breast and dream of steak.

Like the Israelites, I am blessed beyond measure, but I am not always content with God's wonderful gifts.

My life is full of manna from God—daily provision for my every need. My discontent doesn't lie in God's provision. It lives in my attitude toward what He provides.

Every day I have a choice—gratitude or grumbling, delight or despair.

Every day, my choice has consequences—delicious contentment or bitter dissatisfaction. How I view my life is a direct result of my attitude toward God, and when my heart is not thankful, I am in danger of challenging God's sovereignty.

Thankfulness is a command (1 Thessalonians 5:18) to obey as well as a state of the heart that allows me to be content with what God has provided for me. I want to honor God with my choice to obey Him with a thankful heart.

Today, I choose gratitude, and I thank God for His abundant blessings in my life.

Father, You have been so good to me. Every day You provide what I need. Every day you give and give until I can say with the psalmist, "My cup runs over". Forgive me for times when I have failed to thank You, for times when I have been ungrateful. Thank You for your continued faithfulness and goodness. Thank You for the contentment that I find in You.

Think About It:
- What are you most apt to complain about?
- What are you most grateful for?

Grace When I am Tossed About

For the which cause I also suffer these things: nevertheless I am not ashamed: for I know whom I have believed, and am persuaded that he is able to keep that which I have committed unto him against that day.
—2 Timothy 1:12

On our walk to the beach, we braced ourselves against the increasing gusts of wind. Sand streamed across open areas, chased by air that swirled and pushed. As we topped the dune, the froth of crashing waves made whitecaps on water that a few hours ago had been still and calm. A tropical system offshore was becoming evident.

Our walk was shorter than usual due to the wind. Even though the temperature was moderate, our jackets gave welcome warmth and protection from the air chilled by rain, ocean moisture, and breeze. We pulled the door closed behind us, thankful for the protection of sturdy walls and roof.

I thought about that this morning as I read from the first chapter of James. "But let him ask in faith, nothing wavering. For he that wavereth is like a wave of the sea driven with the wind and tossed" (James 1:6).

I saw the tossing of those waves today, and I have felt the tossing that comes from a wavering faith in my soul before.

This verse speaks to stability, to unwavering trust in our Father who loves us with a love so exhaustive that it is undefinable. It speaks to trust. It speaks to relationship.

The more that I know my Father, the more that I know about Him, the more I trust Him. Faith is a firm foundation, but it calls for me to set both feet firmly on the promises and truth of God's Word.

Faith is not an in-and-out proposition. Faith does not pick and choose when and what from the Bible to believe. Faith is all in.

A story is told of a gymnast who perfected the stunt of pushing a wheelbarrow across a high wire. The gymnast performed the stunt without difficulty before an amazed audience. He then chose a man from the audience and asked this question, "Do you believe that I can push this wheelbarrow across the wire without falling?"[9]

The man quickly answered, "Absolutely".

Again, the gymnast questioned the man, "Are you certain?"

The man replied, "I just saw you do it. I am certain."

The gymnast's next statement, however, gave the man pause. "Get in then."

It is easy to talk about what God can do, about His faithfulness and His promises. When trials come, though, when wisdom is needed, we step back. Anxiousness, rather than faith, reigns. We are tossed like the waves of the sea, driven by the wind of trial.

God calls us to stability. He calls us to get into the wheelbarrow and trust Him with every tiny bit of life. Then, when we pray, we pray with the confidence of knowing God, of knowing His care, of knowing His love, of knowing His character.

God calls for us to be all in. Then, when the storms of life begin brewing and the winds of trial buffet our souls, we can remain grounded in Who He is.

Walk in faith today, grounded in the TRUTH of God's Word, for He IS faithful.

"That we henceforth be no more children, tossed to and fro, and carried about with every wind of doctrine, by the sleight of men, and cunning craftiness, whereby they lie in wait to deceive;" (Ephesians 4:14).

Father, I have walked many miles with You, and I know You are trustworthy. I know Your word is true. Still, there are times of trial when I am tossed like those waves on the sea. Forgive my unbelief. Continue to grow me as I study Your word, so that I will be a stable follower of You who can lead others to You. You are a good Father.

Think About It:
- When was a time that you felt tossed about in your faith? What did you do?
- How can you grow stronger in faith?

Running on My Knees

Continue in prayer, and watch in the same with thanksgiving;
—Colossians 4:2

Guilty!

I have said, "All I can do is pray," so many times, with a sigh and a look of resignation.

Praying is the last resort when all my own efforts have proven fruitless. As if beginning to pray means that all is hopeless, and I am going through the motions for a dying cause.

My comment should be a confident, resounding proclamation, "I can pray!"

I can talk to my Father, who is the Lord of the Universe. I can call on the resources of Heaven to meet a need. I can engage in conversation with the Creator.

I can pray!

Prayer is not resignation. It is not the end of the road or a last resort for a Christian. It is my first line of defense in spiritual warfare. Prayer connects me to my Source of power. Prayer opens my heart to God, and prayer is the life breath of the God follower.

We talk about prayer a lot. We do studies on how to pray. We take prayer requests and keep prayer lists, but I wonder how much we actually talk with God.

When Paul tucked those three short words "Pray without ceasing" (1 Thessalonians 5:17) into his list of instructions for the Thessalonian church, he wasn't just filling up space in his letter. He was giving them and us vital instructions on how to survive as Christians in this world.

In Ephesians 6:18, he wraps up the full armor of God by telling us to pray "always with all prayer and supplication in the Spirit" reminding us that we cannot fight the battle alone. We need God's help, God's power.

I don't fully understand prayer, but I do know that praying changes me. Praying realigns my focus and clears my heart. Praying settles my soul when the world is in chaos. Praying connects me to God, and there is no better place to be.

No matter how the circumstances scream for attention, I know that running to the Father is always the best thing for me to do. I can run to Him on my knees.

I can pray!

"Watch and pray, that ye enter not into temptation: the spirit indeed is willing, but the flesh is weak" (Matthew 26:41).

Dear Father, how often I take the privilege of talking with You for granted. How often I try to do things on my own before running to You. It never works, Lord. You have given me a way to communicate with You. May I be faithful in running to You in my heart and on my knees every moment of every day, knowing that only there will I find true victory.

Think About It:
- How often do you pray?
- Do you have a time set aside to talk with the Father?
- Try praying scripture to stimulate your prayer time.

Intercessors

Woven through fragile moments
That glisten with unspoken fears,
Quiet sighs, whispered words,
Unseen tears.

They lift troubled hearts to God,
And plead His love to thwart the cares
Spawned by humanness so frail—
Ceaseless prayers.

Grace to Deal with Questions

But I have trusted Your mercy. My heart will rejoice in Your salvation. I will sing unto the LORD, because He has dealt bountifully with me.
—Psalm 13:5–6

I look for verbs when I am reading scripture—you know, those action words that you learned about in school. I also take note when I see the word "but". This little word signals change or contrast, and it can alert me to a change of heart or action.

I found both grammatical interests while reading Psalm 13.

In the six short verses of this psalm, David pours out the questions plaguing his heart. He wasn't afraid to bring his questions to God, and we should not be either.

David, having survived King Saul's assaults and life in the wilderness, presented four questions.

1. **How long will You forget me, O Lord?** I know that God doesn't forget, and David did, too. There are times, though, when we feel forgotten, when this world knocks us around and we feel far from God's presence. These are times when faith is tested.
2. **How long will You hide Your face from me?** David felt abandoned as he hid from King Saul in the wilderness. The wilderness of this modern-day world can challenge our sense of God's presence as well.
3. **How long will I take counsel in my soul, having sorrow in my heart?** David knew the sorrow of betrayal and physical need. He felt like God just expected him to work it out on his own.

4. **How long will my enemy win?** Can you hear the cries of Christians today in that question? "How long will You let this go on, God." "How long will You wait to stop the wickedness in the world?" "How long do I have to put up with a world view that has erased You?"

I find it interesting that God did not answer David's questions. Instead, we see David aligning his heart with God in the rest of this psalm.

He asks for God to hear him. He knows his enemy will think he has won and will rejoice over his defeat, and David asks God to prevent this. It is almost like David realizes that these are not the things that will shape or destroy his life, though. This is where we see that word "BUT". "But I have trusted Your mercy. My heart will rejoice in Your salvation. I will sing unto the LORD, because He has dealt bountifully with me" (Psalm 13:5–6).

Despite what the world was throwing at him, David chose God. He proved this by taking three actions.

He trusted.

He rejoiced.

He sang.

Simple actions (remember I said I look for verbs) showing that David chose God's way, even in his questioning, over the way of the world. I can almost see David getting up from his knees, brushing himself off, and lifting his head. That "BUT" signaled David's victory over his despair. Three simple actions allowed him to go on in faith.

Those are good actions for me to take today. I may not understand what is going on in our world, and I may not know God's timeline, but I can follow David's example.

- I will trust (lay my whole weight upon) God's mercy. I know He will see me through.

- I will rejoice in His deliverance of my soul from the darkness of the enemy. He has saved me.
- I will praise Him in song, displaying my gratitude for His goodness.

Questions.

We all have them, and I am not sure we would understand the answers if God shouted them from Heaven.

BUT I can trust Him. I can rejoice in Him. I can praise Him.

That will change my day. It can change yours, too.

Father, there are so many things that I do not understand in this world. So many things that are contrary to Your word and Your way. I want them fixed. I know You are able, and I know You have a plan. Today, I choose to trust You with my questions, to lay all my weight on who You are knowing that You are in complete control. I thank You for Your deliverance and for Your salvation. Let me be faithful in sharing Your word. And I praise You for Your everlasting goodness.

Think About It:
- Do you have questions like David?
- Can you trust those questions to the sovereignty of God?

Grace in Every Circumstance

But as for you, ye thought evil against me; but God meant it unto good, to bring to pass, as it is this day, to save much people alive.
—Genesis 50:20

Every day brings new circumstances.

Circumstances can toss us and defeat us, or circumstances can strengthen us. We can use our circumstances as excuses to avoid obeying God or we can allow Him to use us in our circumstances.

Genesis tells us the story of Joseph, a man whose life was fraught with negative circumstances. He was hated by his brothers, sold into slavery, falsely accused, and then thrown into prison. If anyone had reason to complain and despair, it was Joseph. His circumstances were often dismal.

Time and again, however, we see Joseph rising above his circumstances to remain obedient to God. Joseph's story is told in Genesis 37 and continued in chapters 39 through 50. It is a good read.

Joseph proved himself faithful in slavery and was given great responsibility. When falsely accused and thrown into prison, he continued his faithful service. Soon, he was given authority over the everyday workings of the prison. Later, when the butler forgot his promise to speak for Joseph, Joseph did not throw up his hands in despair. Instead, he continued to faithfully serve until God delivered him.

We can easily see God's hand on Joseph's life as we study his story in Genesis, but he must have had trouble tracing God's purpose as he lived out his young life in slavery. He woke every day as a slave, and every day he served God in his slavery. He allowed God to use him and teach him through many years of difficult service before he saw a change in his position.

Circumstances did not rule Joseph's life. God did.

In the vernacular of the sixties, Joseph bloomed where he was planted.[10]

As I read about Joseph's faithfulness, I must consider my own. Do I focus solely on my circumstances of health, or financial needs, or work issues, or family problems each day, or do I act in obedience to God's word? Do I allow hardship to deter my faithfulness? Am I living dependent on what is happening in my life, or am I allowing God to teach me through the daily occurrences?

Good questions to consider, but how can I tell whether I am living in response to my circumstances or despite them?

God has given directions in His word that can give me insight into whether I am obeying Him despite my circumstances or whether I am allowing them to rule my thoughts, attitude, and actions.

Here are a few:

- Do I rejoice in the Lord always? (Philippians 4:4)
- Do I give thanks in all things? (I Thessalonians 5:18)
- Am I allowing my life to be a living sacrifice for Him? (Romans 12:1)
- Am I conforming to the attitudes of the world, or am I allowing His word to transform me? (Romans 12:2)
- Is His love evident in my actions toward others, even those who do not show love to me? (Romans 12:10)
- Do I display patience when things do not go according to my plan? (Romans 12:12)
- Do I bless those who persecute me? (Romans 12:14)
- Are my words filled with grace? (Colossians 4:6)
- Do I seek to overcome evil with good? (Romans 12:21)
- Am I hospitable and generous to others? (Romans 12:13)

Human nature focuses on circumstances. "If my house was nicer, I would have people over. If I had more education, I would talk to others about Christ. If I felt better, I would pray for others. If I was wealthy, I would give. If the people at work were not so difficult, I would befriend them. If I was talented, I would serve God more. If I wasn't so rushed, I would read my Bible. If"—you fill in the blank.

God has called me right where I am, in the circumstances of today, to follow Him. He has called me to trust Him to work through my circumstances to grow me and accomplish His good.

I can, like Joseph, choose to be obedient and faithful, or I can choose to allow circumstances to rule my thoughts and life.

I want to be like Joseph.

How about you?

Father, I confess that there are days that circumstances threaten to overwhelm me, and I let them carry me along like a boat on a river. I want to paddle the boat, though, Lord. Help me to be faithful, to depend on Your strength for each moment. I want to live above my circumstances in the power of Your Holy Spirit. I commit my life to You, Lord, to live in obedience to Your word even when it is not convenient or easy. I trust You to strengthen my heart.

Think About It:
- What circumstances are threatening to overpower you today?
- How can you obey God despite your circumstances?

Seasons of Grace

Seasons of grace
flow year after year
through tears and trial
and loss and laughter.
Carried along streams
of refreshment,
and over hills of endurance,
we travel through the crevices of care
and the potholes of pain.
Autumn's times of harvest
trail behind summer's
growth and labor.
Winter's hardness and shadows thaw into
the glorious promise of spring,
and we hope once again.
Through all the seasons,
God's love writes lyrics of grace
that echo a sonnet of joy
deep within the soul,
and the seasons of the heart
flow on.

Reviving Hope: Grace Lessons From Resilient Ferns

Jesus said unto her, I am the resurrection, and the life: he that believeth in me, though he were dead, yet shall he live:
—John 11:25

I have two huge pots of ferns that have resided under an oak tree in my yard for several years. They are too big to move, so they stay right there through the winter. Usually, the tree is enough to shelter them through most of the cold weather. They die back a little, but not enough to be a problem. I made peace with the fact several years ago that if they die, they die.

Well, this year death happened.

An unusual Florida ice storm was too much for them. They turned into nothing but pots of brown twigs.

Even though I inspected them carefully, I could find no sign of life in those ferns. I reluctantly told my husband that we would just take them and dump them in the woods because I couldn't fix the damage. And that was the plan—several weeks ago.

Imagine my surprise as I walked past the oak tree this week and spotted green shoots popping up amid all those ugly brown stems. What I considered dead still had life in the roots, and the warm spring air was waking that life up.

I thought those ferns were beyond hope, but God knew better.

I wonder how many times I have judged a person as beyond hope, too far gone, ready for the dump, when the warmth of God's love can still stir life in that person. I wonder.

How many people seem like my dead ferns, their spirits broken, easily dismissed, just waiting for God's touch to bring life? Maybe I am the one God is planning to use to touch that life with His love. Hmm.

There were times in scripture when the enemy thought that God's people were defeated, that they couldn't rise again, but God brought them back.

And look at Jesus on the cross. Even the disciples thought all was lost, but three days later—the Resurrection!

We humans have a way of pronouncing things hopeless and dead, but God is all about bringing life.

I know that God brought Life to my soul. I am thankful He didn't think I was too hopeless.

Those ferns reminded me to be careful about declaring plants or people doomed to failure when God is all about Life and all about the impossible. This is true of my own life as well.

In fact, I think that is one of spring's messages.

Father, Spring is a time of new growth and life. We come out of winter seasons cold and broken, but You offer life. You are all about hope, restoration, and grace. Let Your resurrection life be seen in me, Lord. Let me offer the hope of Your resurrection to the broken that I see all around me. I want to celebrate Spring in this world—the Spring of Your life, Your resurrection, no matter what time of year it is. Let it be so.

Think About It:
- Do you have something that you have pronounced hopeless that you need to turn over to God?
- How does Jesus' resurrection bring hope to your life?

Grace to Live by Faith in All Life's Seasons

> *The Lord is my light and my salvation; whom shall I fear? the Lord is the strength of my life; of whom shall I be afraid? When the wicked, even mine enemies and my foes, came upon me to eat up my flesh, they stumbled and fell. Though an host should encamp against me, my heart shall not fear: though war should rise against me, in this will I be confident.*
> —Psalm 27:1–3

Habakkuk is a short, three-chapter Old Testament book by a little-known prophet. We stumble over his name, and we may skip over this tiny book. But Habakkuk had an important message for God's people, and since, "All scripture is given by inspiration of God, and is profitable for doctrine, for reproof, for correction, for instruction in righteousness:" (2 Timothy 3:16), I know that God's truth in this book is relevant for me today.

Habakkuk lived during the time of King Josiah, a time of revival in Israel's history. But the revival was squashed under the ungodly leadership of King Josiah's successor, Jehoiakim. With the breaking of the covenant with God, judgment came, and this was the burden that Habakkuk carried for his people.

Think about that for a moment... a godly heritage, a turning from God's way, the rise of wickedness in the nation. Does any of that sound familiar?

When the book opens, Habakkuk is distraught and questioning. How long will God allow the wickedness to go unchecked? Why does it seem that God does not hear the cry of His people? Why must we see this sin and this sorrow?

Chapter one, verse five seemed to give a little hope when God promised to work a work in Habakkuk's lifetime that he would not believe. However, the work that God would work was judgment. The nation of Israel would be conquered. People and homes and livelihoods would be destroyed. Hard times were ahead.

This was not good news.

As God shared this troubling information with the prophet, He also told Habakkuk what to do. In chapter two, God instructed Habakkuk to write the vision concerning the judgment that was coming. Then God shared a simple truth with Habakkuk, "the just shall live by his faith" (Habakkuk 2:4).

God told Habakkuk to trust Him.

This phrase is repeated in the New Testament (Romans 1:17, Galatians 3:11, Hebrews 10:38), but Habakkuk was the first to pen it.

God called Habakkuk to believe that His word, His provision, His plan was enough, and He calls us to believe the same.

"Live by faith" is an easy phrase to say, but a hard action to maintain. I'm often plagued by questions like, "How do I live by faith when everything is falling apart? What if I can't see the next step? What if the future appears grim? How do I live by faith in seasons of trial?

When I think about living by faith, I think about what that looks like in my daily life.

When I live by faith:

- I no longer base my relationship with God on my own goodness. I trust that He has declared me righteous through His Son.
- I look beyond what I can see and feel, and I live confidently in God's provision and care for me.

- I live life according to the truth revealed in God's Word, even when those around me are living in opposition to God's teaching and are urging me to do the same.
- I base my hope and contentment on God's assured promises of eternity rather than on the temporal circumstances of this life.
- I trust God's timing, and I remember that He is in control.
- I find joy and strength for every day in the reality of Who God is.
- I trust in the promise of tomorrow, regardless of the diagnosis, the political agenda, or the weather forecast, because my trust is in the omnipotent God.

Habakkuk began with questions, but he ended with certainty. The last few verses of the book tell us the end of Habakkuk's story. "Yet I will rejoice in the Lord, I will joy in the God of my salvation. The Lord God is my strength, and he will make my feet like hinds' feet, and he will make me to walk upon mine high places" (Habakkuk 3:18–19).

Habakkuk found joy and strength in God every day.

His circumstances had not changed. Judgment still loomed. His status in life had not changed. Habakkuk's focus, however, had changed. Now, he looked through the eyes of faith in the omnipotent God. Instead of despair, God gave joy and strength.

As I look out at our fractured world today, I want to look with eyes of faith, knowing that God is in control and that He will accomplish His purposes.

What joy and strength I find in Him as He gives me grace to live by faith in all life's seasons.

Father God, my faith is not always strong, and sometimes I let my eyes turn to the circumstances around me. Grant grace that I will keep my eyes on You, always following Your word, always looking toward Your face. You have told me that faith comes through Your word, so keep me faithful in studying Your word. Grow me in the grace and knowledge of You, Lord. You are my joy and strength every day. In Jesus' precious name.

Think About It:
- What does living by faith mean to you?
- When is it hardest for you to live by faith?

Grace During Seasons of Stress

Be careful for nothing; but in every thing by prayer and supplication with thanksgiving let your requests be made known unto God. 7 And the peace of God, which passeth all understanding, shall keep your hearts and minds through Christ Jesus.
—Philippians 4:6–7

Stress.

I hear this word everywhere I go, from everyone I talk with. I experience it in the day-to-day happenings of my life, and I deal with it in the lives of those I love.

A few years ago, I determined a working definition of stress that works for me. See what you think:

- **S** – Seeking
- **T** - To
- **R** - Resolve
- **E** - Every
- **S** - Silly
- **S** – Situation

Now, you might choose to replace the word "silly" with "serious" or some other word, but I don't really think it matters. Stress comes when my expectations do not meet reality, so I continually try to bring the two together.

Not all stress is bad. The realization that reality does not meet my expectation can motivate me to work hard and achieve. It can cause me to think of better solutions to problems. That's good.

But then there's the stress that comes from constantly trying to fix everything for everyone. That stress is not so good.

Stress can be prideful. When I assume I can resolve every problem and fix every issue, I focus on my own strength. God never called me to fix the world, nor did He call me to be the world's quality control manager. He called me to love Him and to allow Him to love others through me. He called me to walk with Him in fellowship – not stress.

He even gave me guidance for stress relief. "Rejoice in the Lord always: and again I say, Rejoice. Let your moderation be known unto all men. The Lord is at hand. Be careful for nothing; but in every thing by prayer and supplication with thanksgiving let your requests be made known unto God. And the peace of God, which passeth all understanding, shall keep your hearts and minds through Christ Jesus" (Philippians 4:4–7).

I find three directions in those verses that are sure antidotes for stress.

- The first one is **joy**. Joy diffuses the tension that builds in difficult situations. It is often controlled by where I choose to place my focus in life—on the circumstance or on the God of the circumstance. There is great truth in the proverb "A merry heart doeth good like a medicine: but a broken spirit drieth the bones" (Proverbs 17:22).
- The second is **prayer**. Prayer says that I know that I am not in charge, but I know Who is. Prayer places my dependence on the only One Who can truly effect change.
- The third is **thanksgiving**. It is difficult to be overcome with stress when I am busy being thankful for the multitude of mercies in my life and in the lives of those around me.

The next verse in Philippians gives me a little more guidance. "Finally, brethren, whatsoever things are true, whatsoever things are honest, whatsoever things are just, whatsoever things are pure, whatsoever things are lovely, whatsoever things are of good report; if there be any virtue, and if there be any praise, think on these things" (Philippians 4:8).

- A fourth antidote to stress—My **thoughts.** My thoughts must focus on the good rather than the bad. This is not a Pollyanna approach to life that never acknowledges sorrow or pain, but it is choosing to meditate on uplifting thoughts rather than purposefully dwelling on the mean, spiteful, hurtful things of life. It is moving past the difficult, horrifying memories to remember kindness, mercy, laughter, and grace. Sometimes, this means that I must control what (or whom) I spend my time listening to, watching, and reading. You know the old saying—junk in, junk out. And guess what. One of the fruits of the Spirit is self-control, so we can have the Holy Spirit's help with this.

This life is stressful. The overwhelming expectations that come from the constant bombardment of information, as well as the daily trials that I face, can cause my soul to buckle under the strain. But I have a fortress, a strength, a refuge that can shelter me and allow me to face each day with confidence and joy when I use God's remedies.

Father, it seems like some days I am all about silly situations. I stress myself out over every little thing that comes up, instead of resting in Your strength. Teach me to turn to You, to rely on You, to lean on You, to find my joy in You. Help me to control my thoughts, Father. Ground me in Your word, for it is true and pure. You are my light and my salvation. Forgive me for allowing myself to be caught in the minutia of daily madness. Teach me, soul, to be still in You. Remind me to laugh today, Lord. In Jesus' name I pray.

Think About It:
- What silly situations are you struggling with in this season of your life?

- How can you release these into God's hands?
- What is something you can give thanks for today?
- What is something you can laugh about today?

Keeper of My Heart

Sometimes darkness creeps up on my soul,
entering the crevasses of my heart and troubling my mind.
I notice the spinning thoughts, the obsession with problems,
the oppressive spirit that weighs me down,
and I know it is time—
Time to walk outside into the whirling, drifting colors.
Time to allow my mind to wander through floating clouds
and dive into the endless blue sky.
Time to listen to a rippling stream or the brush of sea on sand,
to be still in the wonder of God's creation and remember—
My Creator planned and pieced this mighty creation.
My Father has not forgotten His creation,
nor has He lost me in its vastness.
My Sovereign Lord is still on the throne,
and He is attentive to His children.
My Omnipotent God will honor His promises and keep His covenants.
My life is inextricably hidden in His love for eternity.
Evil will not win.
Death will not conquer.
When the skirmishes and battles are done,
victory is sure.
Until then,
He will keep my heart.

Grace that Gives Joy in All Seasons of Life

Rejoice in the Lord always: and again, I say, Rejoice.
—Philippians 4:4

There are seasons in my life that I find myself parked in certain parts of the scripture. Passages that seem to speak grace to my soul and fill me up regardless of the circumstances I am facing.

The fourth chapter of Philippians is one of those parking lots.

I keep going back there. Morning after morning. Day after day.

The message resonates in my soul, and I keep trying to grasp it. Hold it close. Because I know there is strength in the words that God gave Paul to pen. I know there is hope and grace there that can buoy my faith as I wade through the floodwaters that often threaten to overflow.

Paul was in prison. In prison. He had suffered so much. And yet this is what God told him to write. "Rejoice in the Lord always: and again I say, Rejoice" (Philippians 4:4).

Prison is not a good place to be. Paul was confined. His freedom was stripped from him, yet God told him to rejoice and to tell the people in the Philippian church to do the same.

But wait, they were not supposed to just jump around and pretend to be happy. The command was specific. They were to rejoice in the Lord.

Take joy in who God is. Rejoice in Him always, no matter what is happening in this life—even prison.

This is a command, and as with all God's commands, it is for our good. It will require effort, because it does not come naturally. How much easier it is to roll around in the muck and the mud than to look up and find joy in the Lord.

But make no mistake. The joy is there.

It whispers in the breeze across the rooftop. It lingers in the smile that passes in the hospital hallway. You can catch it in the sigh of rest at the end of a long day or in the wakening light of morning. Sometimes it rests in the stillness of the heart that reminds you He is near.

Stop the mumbling and the worry. Stop the incessant complaining. For this moment, rejoice in the amazing glory of who God is. Take joy in the redemption that Christ has provided.

Realize that eternity is in this minute, and He is here.

That is joy.

Even in prison.

What is your prison today? Is it illness? Financial difficulty? A relationship? Sorrow? Whatever it is, God is calling you to rejoice in Him.

Not in the situation, but in who He is. In His almighty presence, His love, His grace, His mercy, His faithfulness.

That's what Paul did.

Allow God's grace to turn this season of your life into a season of joy.

Father, You are my joy. From the innermost part of my being, Your joy bubbles like a spring in my soul. There are times when I allow the world's debris to clog that spring and I struggle to find Your joy. Forgive me, Lord. Focus my heart and eyes on You this moment and this day. Remind me how wonderful You are. I thank You for Your marvelous grace and Your sweet forgiveness. I trust You with the pain and sorrow in my life. I trust You to open the doors of the prisons that try to hold me fast. You are my Lord, and I cherish You. In Jesus's precious name I joyously pray.

Think About It:
- What is your prison today?
- Spend some time thinking about what God has done and thanking Him. Then check your joy meter. Is it higher than before?

Grace in Seasons of Crisis

As soon as Jesus heard the word that was spoken, he saith unto the ruler of the synagogue, Be not afraid, only believe.
—Mark 5:36

Jairus was a well-known man, a ruler of synagogue. His story is told in the fifth chapter of Mark, verses 21 through 36. He may have been an important man, but he was also a dad. And on the day that he came to Jesus seeking help for his critically ill daughter, his world was crashing around him.

Everyone told Jairus it was no use. "Don't bother talking to Jesus. Your daughter is dead." But Jesus' only words to him were "Don't be afraid; only believe" (Mark 5:36). Jesus didn't promise to heal the daughter. He didn't give him any real hope. Just two seemingly simple tasks, except for the fact those tasks were tied up in the fate of his daughter.

After Jairus had found Jesus and Jesus had agreed to come with him to his daughter's bedside, Jesus stopped along the way to minister to a woman who had been ill for many years. The Bible doesn't say, but I can almost feel Jairus' impatience to get to his daughter. He may have even been angry with Jesus for not hurrying when they were met by the messengers who relayed that Jairus' daughter had died.

It was at that moment, however, that Jesus required something of Jairus—"Don't be afraid; only believe." The very second that his world came crushing down—refuse fear and choose to trust. The time when Satan threw his arsenal of doubt darts—refuse fear and choose to trust.

These are the same words God speaks to us when we stand in the middle of unspeakable horror, numbing sorrow, and debilitating

disease. When our world is collapsing around us and our minds cannot comprehend the next step, He gives us two seemingly simple tasks:
- refuse fear
- choose to trust.

Refuse to see things from the world's perspective. Refuse to focus on the problem without considering the resurrection power of Christ. Refuse fear.

Remember the unwavering devotion of the Father who loves you. Remember the grace that shines through life's darkest moments. Remember the omnipotent power of the Creator God. Choose to trust.

We are living through days of confusion and unease. Threatened by turmoil and pestilence and facing uncertain times, we struggle to maintain a positive outlook. But God requires us, just as He required Jairus, to refuse fear and choose to trust.

This doesn't mean that we stop working and just sit. But it does mean that we allow faith rather than fear to control our thoughts and attitudes. We refuse to be paralyzed by fear. We see hope through the lens of faith. We see blessing in the everyday miracles of love and support.

In His time and in His way, Jesus addressed Jairus' need. Others were ministered to and helped along the way. Jairus experienced trusting God when he didn't know the outcome.

In our darkest moments, God calls us to trust Him. Always, in His time and in His way, God overcomes the darkness with His light.

Refuse fear.

Choose to trust.

These are the tasks that give us grace to maneuver through whatever crisis we face.

"For I know whom I have believed, and am persuaded that he is able to keep that which I have committed unto him against that day" (2 Timothy 1:12).

Father, today let me not respond from fear or hurt, but from the foundation of Your overwhelming love, which sought me, bought me, and holds me unconditionally in the safe haven of Your care. Grant Your strength when I am weak and Your steady arm when I am prone to stumble. I choose to trust You. Let Your light shine through. In the strong name of Jesus I pray.

Think About It:
- What is a crisis where you have had to refuse fear and choose to trust?
- When is it hardest for you to do this?

Grace that Lives in Gratitude

In every thing give thanks: for this is the will of God in Christ Jesus concerning you.
—1 Thessalonians 5:18

I have read the first chapter of Romans many times.

While it begins with Paul's greetings to the Roman Christians and his declaration of the power of the gospel of Jesus Christ (verse 16), the overall tone is not a happy one. This chapter speaks to the lostness of mankind and the depths to which our sin carries us.

A short phrase in verse twenty-one, however, caught my attention in a recent reading. I have cruised through this phrase before, but this time it hit me in the heart. "Because that, when they knew God, they glorified Him not as God, neither were thankful; but became vain in their imaginations, and their foolish heart was darkened" (Romans 1:21).

Right in the middle of that verse are three words—neither were thankful. What is that doing there? That seems pretty mild to be specifically pointed out at the beginning of a long description of mankind's degradation.

"Neither were thankful."

As I thought on that phrase, though, I realized—being unthankful, a lack of gratitude, speaks to a state of heart, and the slippery slope to destruction starts in the heart.

Unthankful means:
- I feel and act as though I am entitled.
- I am at the center of my universe.
- I am not recognizing my dependence on the mercy of God.
- I see myself as superior to others.

"Unthankful" sets one up for a tremendous fall.

I thought about other verses in scripture where God commands me to be thankful.

"Giving thanks always for all things unto God and the Father in the name of our Lord Jesus Christ" (Ephesians 5:20).

"And let the peace of God rule in your hearts, to the which also ye are called in one body; and be ye thankful" (Colossians 3:15).

"O give thanks unto the Lord, for he is good: for his mercy endureth for ever" (Psalm 107:1). (These exact words are repeated numerous times in scripture.)

Thankfulness to God is a theme that runs through the entire Bible, and it is a defining characteristic of the believer. It is God's will for my life. Thankfulness means that I see me in the light of who God is. I recognize my unworthiness and His Sovereignty. A thankful heart is ready to worship, ready to give. Gratitude is the foundation of humility.

Gratitude is not just a response to good things that happen in my life. It is the attitude of gratefulness for all that God is and all that God does regardless of the circumstances in my life. Gratitude allows me to give thanks in all things, even when the trials are hard and the days are dark, because I know that God is good.

The grace of gratitude carries me through difficult seasons with contentment.

Jesus modeled gratitude when He gave thanks for five small loaves of bread and two fish before He fed the five thousand. He modeled gratitude when He gave thanks for the bread and wine at the last supper. We teach our children to say "please" and "thank you" because we want them to be polite. This is wonderful, but perhaps we should also focus on modeling an "attitude of gratitude" for them in our everyday actions and words.

When an "attitude of gratitude" rules my heart, it also rules my life.

- Gratitude does not dwell with surliness.

- Gratitude does not dwell with self-centeredness.
- Gratitude does not dwell with discontent.

For me, it's heart-check time. Am I thankful to God for His mercy and grace and faithful provision? Does my life reflect thankfulness in how I react to others?

Father, You are so, so good. You are love. You are hope. You are gracious. Thank You for redeeming me. Thank You for keeping me. Thank You for Your marvelous daily provision. Thank You for the joy of knowing and walking with You. Forgive me for the times I have been unthankful. Help my heart and life show my gratitude every day. In Jesus' glorious name I pray.

Think About It:
- In what ways does your life reflect thankfulness?
- Do your actions display gratitude daily?
- What can you do today to grow an attitude of gratitude?

Grace in Seasons of Anxiety

Casting all your care upon him; for he cares for you.
1 Peter 5:7

What do you do when the pressures and darkness of this world overwhelm your soul, when each breath is an effort, and your mind has declared war on your peace?

How do you press on through the swamp of anxiety that defies explanation? How do you take the next step?

Christians are not immune to attacks of despair, but we do have weapons in our arsenal that can help us survive and even declare victory in these most challenging times.

God has instructed us to "put on", or to avail ourselves of His whole armor (Ephesians 6:10-11). While Christians are secure in our place as His children, we must choose to use His protection and His weapons against the forces of evil that attack, and make no mistake, overwhelming anxiety is an attack.

Here are some weapons or antidotes against anxiety that God, in His grace, provides for us:

- **Give thanks.** This seems so simplistic, but our minds are wired such that gratitude and anxiety cannot coexist. Giving thanks is not random; it is purposeful. It may require a pen and paper to force the mind to focus on God as our Source and what is good and right, rather than on the darkness (1 Thessalonians 5:28).

Thank You, God, that I can breathe.
Thank You, God, that the sun came up this morning.
Thank You, God, that... You get the idea.

Start as small as you need to and get as big as you can with your gratitude. Then watch God begin to work in your thoughts and heart.

- **Offer praise.** We can become so frazzled in our anxiety that we forget to praise God. Praise takes us out of ourselves and focuses on Who God is. Praise removes our focus from the problem and places it on the One who can solve the problem. He is the Creator. He is all-powerful. He is Grace. He is Love. (Hebrews 13:15; Ephesians 5:19)
- **Claim God's Promises.** God has promised to keep us and care for us. We can pray His promises when we are in need. *"Father, thank You that You care for me. I am not sure how to pray for relief from this anxiety, so please pray for me (Romans 8:26). You have not given me the spirit of fear, and I ask that this fear be relieved (2 Timothy 1:7). You have promised peace when I bring my anxiety to you—I ask for peace (Philippians 4:6-7). Keep my heart and my mind. You are my Father, and I love You."*
- **Focus Your Thoughts.** We do not have to think only of the bad and difficult things of this life. God has told us where to focus our thoughts. "Finally, brethren, whatsoever things are true (God's Word is true), whatsoever things are honest (God's love is honest), whatsoever things are just (God is just), whatsoever things are pure (God is pure; viewing nature can be pure, listening to children can be pure), whatsoever things are lovely (view a sunrise or a flower), whatsoever things are of good report (things that are worthy of praise); if there be any virtue, and if there be any praise, think on these things" (Philippians 4:8).
- **Trust God.** Again, this seems simplistic, but faith is a powerful shield (Ephesians 6:16) against the anxiety that attacks the soul. "Being confident of this very thing, that He which has begun a good work in you will perform it until the day of Jesus Christ" (Philippians 1:6). God will see you through!
- **PRAY.** This could be at the top of the list. Prayer is our contact with our heavenly Father. This world is hard, and we need this constant link to Him (Ephesians 6:18).

We do not become proficient with these weapons without practice. Just like a soldier with his armor, we must rehearse using them to combat the attacks of anxiety. Our faith muscles grow as we pray God's word and praise Him in the dark times of our lives.

Satan wants us to think that we are alone in this battle. He attempts to isolate us, but God calls us to Himself for protection, for grace, for relief, for peace.

Dear Father, You alone can still my anxious mind and heart. So many things in this life trouble me and cause me to tremble. I am strong only when I stand in You. I can breathe only when I breathe in You. I know You hold me, and You hold this world. You also hold all the pieces of my life and my loved ones' lives. I choose to trust You with everything dear to me, Lord, because I love You, and I know You are good. You are my Shepherd. Lead me beside still waters. Restore my soul. I am safe in Your care. With You, I shall not want. Thank You for taking my cares. In Jesus' holy name I pray.

Think About It"
- What causes you the most anxiety?
- When are you the most anxious?
- What are three verses that you can claim when you are anxious?
- What are three things that you can give thanks for?
- What are three things you can praise God for?

Grace for Seasons of Waiting

But none of these things move me, neither count I my life dear unto myself, so that I might finish my course with joy, and the ministry, which I have received of the Lord Jesus, to testify the gospel of the grace of God.
—Acts 20:24

Wait is a four-letter word.

We cringe when we hear it. Whether we are on the phone and we have to "hold" (another four-letter word) or sitting in a doctor's office or standing in the line at the supermarket, waiting is not our strong suit. We opt for the fast pass, fast food, preorders, anything to avoid the "wait."

Funny, isn't it, that so many of God's people had to wait. Abraham waited until he was almost one hundred before the son of the promise, Isaac, was born. David waited years after Samuel anointed him before he could claim the throne. God's people waited for hundreds of years for the Messiah, and most did not recognize Him when he came.

The book of Acts records an interesting story about the Apostle Paul, who had to endure a time of waiting. After actively travelling and witnessing for the Lord for years, Paul, the Apostle, was accused by the religious leaders in Jerusalem and placed in custody. In Acts 23:11, God confirmed that Paul would go to Rome as His witness. After this assurance from God, many things happened to Paul before he ever reached Rome. Things that required him to wait:

- An armed regiment escorted him to Caesarea so he could testify before the governor, Felix.
- Felix had him wait in jail while the Jews who were accusing him were traveling from Jerusalem.

- After Paul's testimony before Felix, Felix kept Paul detained in Caesarea for two years while he waited for the arrival of Festus.
- Festus, after hearing Paul's case, referred him to King Agrippa, who finally sent him on his way to Rome.

The delays were not over, however. Paul boarded a ship as a prisoner (remember, he had done nothing wrong), and the ship encountered a hurricane. The hurricane blew the ship 476 miles off course before grounding it off the island of Malta.

While on the island of Malta, a viper bit Paul, but Paul was unharmed. Another three months passed before the ship's master was able to secure passage on a ship out of Alexandria, and they continued on their way to Rome.

Waiting time. Delays. Difficulties.

We want to serve God, but life keeps happening. We wonder about God's purpose.

During Paul's delays, he witnessed before four rulers, and we have no idea how many soldiers and guards heard the gospel because of Paul's testimony. He encouraged and preached to 275 souls aboard the ship. He carried the gospel to the island of Melita, where there was no known witness. Paul prayed for the island people, and many were healed. In each city the ship visited, Paul sought out believers to encourage and teach.

Paul eventually reached Rome just as God had promised, but God seemed to have had great plans for the journey as well.

Where we see delays and hardship (woe is me), God sees opportunities to reach people who need Him. Paul faithfully used his waiting time to honor and serve the Lord.

I, too, have a choice. I can huff and squirm at inconveniences and detours, or I can look around me for the opportunities God provides.

God is not about efficiency. He is about people and redemption, regardless of my schedule and timeline.

Wherever I am today, in the office or the grocery store, whatever the situation, God has a task for me. May I be faithful to fulfill it.

Father, let me see past my plan and my destination to the people around me and the journey that You have me on. Open my eyes to see the opportunities You provide. Open my heart to seize Your opportunities. Please help me not to let my schedule get in the way of Your will. Forgive me for becoming frustrated in the waiting. Help me to see potential when You tell me to wait. In the name of our Savior, Jesus, I pray.

Think About It:
- Are you in a waiting season now?
- How does waiting time fit into God's plan?
- How is God using this waiting time in your life?

Grace for Impossible Seasons

And Moses said unto the people, Fear ye not, stand still, and see the salvation of the Lord, which he will show to you to day: for the Egyptians whom ye have seen to day, ye shall see them again no more for ever. The Lord shall fight for you, and ye shall hold your peace.
—Exodus 14:13–14

Life attacks fast and furiously.

Some seasons throw everything, from the stopped-up kitchen sink to flat tires on the car to critical health issues, at us. Sometimes all we can do is duck and dodge as one crisis after another overwhelms, and fear and doubt hover seeking entrance into the soul.

Will things ever calm down? Am I going to make it?

As I read the first part of the book of Exodus, I thought, *the Israelites must have felt this way.* In a matter of a few weeks, they witnessed the plagues of Egypt as God and Moses dealt with Pharaoh, all the while continuing to perform hard slave labor that became increasingly intense. They saw the water turn to blood, and they witnessed the frogs and the lice. Even though God protected them from the plagues, they watched the misery of the Egyptians under God's judgment. As Pharaoh became angrier at God, Pharaoh took his anger out on them.

Then Moses gave instructions for the time of the Passover, and they busily prepared in accordance with God's plan. They waited through the night as death touched the firstborn children in the Egyptian families. I'm sure they heard the wailing and anguish.

As morning dawned and a grief-stricken Pharaoh issued the release for them to travel, they hurriedly gathered and began the trek into the wilderness. Over 600,000 men plus women, children, and livestock followed Moses out of Egypt. Egypt may not have been the most pleasant place for them, but Egypt was what they were used to and what they knew. When they left it, they left their comfort zone.

Not many days passed before the Egyptian army took up chase to overtake them. Even though their numbers were great, and they were walking in God's promise, the Israelites were shaken at the sight. They accused Moses of bringing them into the wilderness to die.

Pharaoh's army was behind them, and the Red Sea was in front of them. They felt trapped and hopelessly out of control. They railed against their situation, and Moses spoke words of wisdom to calm them. These words are recorded in Exodus 14:13–14, and they are good for us today.

1. **Fear not**. This command, so often repeated in scripture, is the first step in overcoming a seemingly hopeless situation. Fear paralyzes. Fear strips us of hope and faith. God is not surprised by our calamity, and we can depend on Him no matter how dire the situation.
2. **Stand still.** When facing a crisis, we often react frantically. Though counter to our natural inclinations, stillness allows us to hear God's voice and see how He is working.
3. **Hold your peace (be quiet).** Words spoken in fear and desperation are often filled with lies. They reinforce the doubt that is attacking the heart. The Israelites demonstrated this when they told Moses that it would have been better if they had stayed in Egypt than to be in their present situation. Moses assured them that God would fight for them. There was no need to fear.

As Moses spoke to calm the Israelites, God spoke to Moses. The Egyptian army was bearing down on their position, and Moses needed the next step. God had not changed His plan for the Israelites.

Regardless of the army and the Red Sea, God was still sending His people forward (Exodus 14:15).

Forward was the Red Sea. To go forward, they had to take God at His word and walk in faith. They had to step into the water.

We can look back and know that this was the best plan for them, but they saw an impossible situation.

Today, no matter how devastating the situation we face may be, we can choose faith over fear. Then, as we quiet our hearts before God, He gives us the next step. The step may seem intolerable, just like the Red Sea seemed terrible to the Israelites, but as we hold our peace and follow Him, we will see His work, His redemption, as He uses us for His purpose and His glory.

What impossible circumstances are you facing in this season of your life? Are you paralyzed by fear, or are you consciously choosing to trust God's hand and move forward? God can make a way when we cannot see a way.

He is good like that.

Father, today is a day of impossible situations. Challenges overwhelm, and my human reasoning cannot untangle the threads to make everything right. But You can. Help me trust You. Help me wait for You, fully expecting to see You part the waters in my life. You have done it before, and I know You can do it today. Thank You for being the Lord of my intolerable challenges.

Think About It:
- What impossible situation are you facing?
- How can you choose faith over fear?
- Is God showing you a way to move forward?

Grace to Continue

Seek the Lord and his strength, seek his face continually.
1 Chronicles 16:11

Continually is a powerful word. What we do continually strongly impacts who we are. Habits are formed by what we do repeatedly, and we build lives on what we persistently do.

We recognize this in the descriptions assigned to people. We can even change an action into a title.

- One who farms – farmer.
- One who teaches – teacher.
- One who complains – complainer.
- One who gossips – gossiper.
- One who attacks – attacker.
- One who worships – worshiper.

I could go on, but I think you get the drift. We are known by what we do continually. Proverbs 20:11 says it like this, "Even a child is known by his doings, whether his work be pure, and whether it be right."

People use our actions to describe us—for good or bad.

In Psalm 71 we see some good things that David did continually. Even in a time of great trouble near the end of his life, he recognized that there were important things about which he needed to be diligent. They are scattered throughout this psalm.

- In verse three, we find his desire to *continually* resort to God. He knew that God was his fortress, and he was determined to run to his place of safety—God.

- In verse six, David determined that his praise would *continually* be of God. No matter what hardships or disappointment he faced, he determined to praise God, *continually*.
- Finally, in verse fourteen, David set his mind to hope *continually*. God had saved him and kept him through the years. Hope in God would counter the despair in his life.

Reading this psalm made me wonder. What would my life be like if I committed to these three actions, continually?

- What if I always (continually) resorted to God? What if He was the first one I sought in trouble or happiness? What if I ran to Him before I consulted a friend, or a self-help book, or Dr. Phil? What if?
- What if I praised God continually? What if I praised Him when things were going my way and when they were not? What if I constantly recognized His power, His goodness, His mercy, His provision, His...? What if I just delighted in giving thanks to my Father, continually? What if?
- What if I set my heart to hope continually? What if I chose hope over despair in the dark times of my life? Knowing that *faith is the substance of things hoped for* (Hebrews 11:1), what if I exercised my faith to hope, continually. What if?

Remember, our actions describe us and what we do continually impacts who we are.

As a follower of Jesus Christ, I want to run to God and praise Him and hope in Him, continually.

Three things:
1. Resort to God
2. Praise Him
3. Hope in Him

The key is continually.
Life-changing!

Father, I want my continual actions to honor You, to build habits that grow me into a strong servant for You. I want to run to You and praise You and hope in You with everything I am and everything I have, continually. Help me to stay focused on You, Lord. Every moment of every day. In Jesus' precious name I pray.

Think About It:
- What or whom do you tend to resort to when you have a problem?
- When is it hardest for you to hope in God?

Place of Grace

When my heart struggles to find the light,
when darkness deepens, and wrong seems right—
I know a refuge, I know a place
where I find truth, and I find grace.

When I am blown by the winds of doubt,
When waves of fear toss my soul about—
I know a refuge, I know a place
where I find peace in my Savior's grace.

When my heart cries for help and ease,
His gracious heart hears my earnest plea.
He pulls me into His sweet embrace—
There I find mercy, and I find grace.

Grace for the Pruning Season

Now no chastening for the present seems to be joyous, but grievous: nevertheless afterward it yields the peaceable fruit of righteousness unto them which are exercised thereby.
—Hebrews 12:11

I have been scrutinizing the garden lately. Pulling up overcrowded plants. Deadheading old blooms to make way for new ones. Trimming small branches that are growing awry. Pruning is not my favorite garden task, but I am working on it.

When something "looks" healthy, I hate to bother it. I dislike clipping branches, pulling plants from crowded planters, snipping roots from rootbound plants. I always wonder if the plants will survive my ministrations. So, too often, I let things alone, ignoring their need for gardening interference.

Even when the planter is too crowded for the plant to continue healthy growth. Even when the bush has limbs growing in unfortunate places. Even when stable growth requires removing parts of the plant that are sapping the nutrients.

But when the plant begins to falter, as evidenced by yellowing leaves or stunted flowers, I suck in my breath, and I intervene with my pruning shears. Unfortunately, by this time, the pruning requires more severe attention, and the plant needs extra attention to survive. And sometimes it doesn't.

I have retreated to my desk now because I know there is more pruning to do outside. I hate pruning.

As I sit here, I think about the verses in John 15:1-4:

> I am the true vine, and my Father is the husbandman. Every branch in me that beareth not fruit he taketh

away: and every branch that beareth fruit, he purgeth it, that it may bring forth more fruit. Now ye are clean through the word which I have spoken unto you. Abide in me, and I in you. As the branch cannot bear fruit of itself, except it abide in the vine; no more can ye, except ye abide in me.

Jesus is the Gardener who prunes the unsightly growth from my life. Thankfully, He does not hate pruning, and He gives His attention to keeping His branches healthy and productive. He cares about my spiritual well-being.

I am really good at cluttering my planter (life) with too many activities that sap the nutrients from my soul. I easily allow habits to hang on like drooping branches and weeds of sin to crowd out the fruit in my life.

Just like my plants need me (poor things), I need my Master Gardener to work in the soil of my soul—daily. Only His Spirit can keep my spirit growing and healthy. Only His work can empower me to do the work He has for me and to bear fruit for His glory.

His pruning is not always comfortable for me, but I know it is necessary if I am to bear good fruit.

I have a part in this. My part is to trust my Gardener when His Spirit convicts me of sin. My part is to yield obediently to the teachings in His Word. My part is to abide in Him, always conscious of His presence and His Lordship of my life. My job is to rest in Him, enjoying the abundant life that He alone provides.

While my own efforts at pruning sometimes do not end well, His pruning always produces the peaceable fruit of righteousness (Hebrews 12:11).

Father, As I read Your word, my own pettiness and faults are brought to light. Actions from years before pop into my mind, and I suddenly realize that they were against You. I'm sorry, Lord. Sorry for the times I walked in self-righteousness, focused on the outside rather than the heart; Sorry for the desire for material things that clouded Your purpose for me; Sorry for bitter thoughts, judgmental attitudes, and self-centeredness; Sorry for making decisions in my own wisdom. I know You have saved me, but sometimes I still let wrong attitudes and actions accumulate and clutter my relationship with You. Prune away the mess, Lord. Let me bear fruit for You. Thank you for the good work you do. In Your Son's strong name I pray.

Think About It:
- What pruning is God doing in your life?
- How do you react to God's pruning?

Grace for Seasons of Learning

*Lead me in thy truth, and teach me: for thou art the God of my
salvation; on thee do I wait all the day.*
—Psalm 25:5

Some seasons of my life seem filled with lessons that God is teaching me. While some people would call them times of trial, I prefer to think of these days as school days. As we have walked through challenging days recently, these are a few lessons that I have been learning. Perhaps you can relate.

Lesson 1: I am not in control. (My head does not think I want to be in control, but my actions disprove what my head thinks. I hate it when that happens!) I set my mind on how things ought to be, and then when they do not work that way, I am upset, which is a lighter word for mad. I try to figure out where I went wrong, and I usually spend countless hours thinking of ways to maneuver the situation to meet my original plan. The maneuverings seldom work, so I am left frustrated (another light word for mad) and disillusioned. Somewhere in this whole scenario, I want to know why God did not answer my prayers the way I wanted, to achieve my plan.

The reality, though, is I am not in charge. God is. Therefore, the only way to live is to commit my way to God and trust Him with the details. I know that He is more than able and willing to handle the details. This brings me to the next lesson He is teaching.

Lesson 2: Things happen. Good things and bad things. I don't usually question the good things, but evil happenings are hard to take. However, in this world ruled by man's free will and the presence of evil, bad things happen. The bad things are not from God (James 1:17), and I know that He is in the middle of every mess working to bring good to His children (Romans 8:28). I often do not understand His working, but God, Himself, is well beyond my human ability to understand.

I do not have to explain everything that happens. I do not have to issue a treatise on the whys and the wherefores. I do not even have to understand. God calls me to trust Him and to follow Him, and that is a full-time job.

While I don't understand the why of many things, I do trust the absolute goodness of God. That way, when caught in the web of the bad, I can cry and run to my Father. Trusting His absolute goodness and love, not just acknowledging them in words, keeps my relationship with Him open. Otherwise, I slam the door on His support and grace and find myself struggling to keep my head up in the bog of this world. When I trust Him, my eyes open to His glorious working in difficulty and despair. Bad things don't disappear, but His goodness and love shine through them.

Lesson 3: Mercy triumphs over judgment. This truth comes from James 2:13. Mercy triumphs! I love that idea, but my humanness defaults to judgment. I don't know why; I just know that no matter what situation I face, I immediately begin to make judgments about right and wrong, about what should be, about accountability. God, however, operates in mercy, compassion, and forgiveness.

There is another lesson closely linked here. I can't see the whole picture. While I can see what is in front of me, I can't see the back story. Therefore, my perceptions and my judgment are skewed. There is no way around this, and that's why I must trust God with the judgment. Only He can see everything, the beginning and the end. Only He can rule and judge in righteousness.

What if my default changed to mercy? How would my attitudes toward people and myself change? God is teaching me, and I am trying to learn, that my most important first reaction is mercy. Mercy is what He gives (Psalm 86:15), and I can leave the judgment to Him.

Lesson 4: Love trumps it all. The closer that I draw to my Father, the more I realize Love. Love is Who He is (1 John 4:8). Love that sacrifices for the good of another, even in the face of rejection. Love that shows mercy. Love that takes the extra step. Love that takes joy in the good that comes to others. Love that demonstrates itself in action. When I think about plans for the future, what I should or should not do, Love must be the qualifying factor. What would Love do?

These are just a few lessons in a season of learning. As we draw near Him, the Holy Spirit is always teaching us and growing us to be more like our Savior. Our school days won't end until we are home with Him.

"But the Comforter, which is the Holy Ghost, whom the Father will send in my name, he shall teach you all things, and bring all things to your remembrance, whatsoever I have said unto you" (John 14:26).

Father, thank you for teaching me how to live life for and with You. Thank You helping me to grow through Your word and through the trials of this life. Help me to be a good student, Lord. In Jesus' name I pray.

Think About It:
- What lessons is God teaching you in this season of your life?
- How is He teaching you? Through trial? Through His word? Through others?

Grace is My Credential for All Seasons

But God forbid that I should glory, save in the cross of our Lord Jesus Christ, by whom the world is crucified unto me, and I unto the world.
—Galatians 6:14

We believe in credentials.

We pad our resumes with our education, experience, and awards. We need others to know how prepared we are for the tasks we face, and we check the credentials of others before we trust them with jobs and services. Credentials are important, and they give us information that allows us to begin to trust someone.

Still, we often feel unworthy. When faced with a new responsibility, our hearts quiver because deep down inside, we know all those qualifications do not completely define who we are. We know our inadequacies, our insecurities, our weaknesses. We know our flaws.

The Apostle Paul felt unworthy. He called himself the least of all the apostles (1 Corinthians 15:9). Why? Because he knew his past—he had persecuted the church of God. He didn't trust Christ during Christ's earthly ministry. He came after the fact, after the resurrection, after the birthing of the church, after walking in rebellion, after God knocked him down on the road to Damascus.

While we read his resume in Philippians 4:6–8 and think, "Wow", Paul knew his education and training did not measure up to Christ.

This is why I love how Paul introduces himself in the first verse of Galatians.

"Paul, an apostle, (not of men, neither by man, but by Jesus Christ, and God the Father, who raised him from the dead;)" (Galatians 1:1).

Paul didn't hand out copies of his resume to the Galatians. He didn't qualify himself through education or experience. He simply stated that God had made him an apostle. His ministry was God's, and his authority rested on God's work in his life.

God has given me credentials just like He gave them to Paul.

When Satan calls me unworthy, I can pull out my diplomas and awards and wave them around, but they won't scare him off. However, when I acknowledge God's work in my life, Satan is speechless. He has no way to contradict the redeeming power of Christ.

I, like Paul, do not stand on my own merit but on the worthiness of Christ, my Savior. I do not serve in my own strength but in the mighty strength of my Father.

My credentials bear His name because I am His work.

So, while experience, education, and training have a place on resumes and in this life, I must remember that I am here because of God. He qualified and called me. I may feel unworthy, but He has made me worthy through the atoning sacrifice and resurrection of Jesus Christ His Son. I am a daughter of the King.

This truth allows me, like Paul, to walk with confidence and to serve Him with assurance.

If you know Christ, you, too, can live with the knowledge that you are accepted in the Beloved (Philippians 1:6) and you are no longer unworthy to serve Him.

Father, I stand before you known. There is nothing hidden. You know everything, and you love me still. You have called me and redeemed me just as You did Paul. This fact blows me away. You have qualified me for the work to which I am called. May I be as faithful as Paul. May I honor you as Paul did. You have taken away my condemnation and declared me free and clean and worthy. Thank you, Jesus, for the blood you shed. Thank you.

Think About It:
- Are there areas of your life that you struggle with feelings of unworthiness?
- How can we keep from becoming prideful when we know that Christ has taken away our condemnation?

Saving Grace

Restless, mankind ever seething,
Seeking power to have control,
Striking out against the Master
Who alone redeems the soul.

Through the ages kings have crumbled
As they shook their fists at Him,
Always thinking they could conquer,
Relishing the depths of sin.

Violently, the battle rages
As the end of time draws near.
Satan's army always grasping
To pull souls into his lair.

But the Master, Overcomer,
Still commands the battle strong.
He has crowned His Son in honor.
He will sing the victor's song.

Give your hearts to Him, oh people.
Fear this One Who is the Lord.
Place your trust in His redemption,
Leaning wholly on His Word.

Grace for the Lost

But as many as received him, to them gave he power to become the sons of God, even to them that believe on his name:
—John 1:12

Lost!

Such a terrifying word!

In the past weeks and months, I have lost my prescription sunglasses, my keys, my Bible, and a hotel key. Looking back over a few years, I have lost my wallet, a business checkbook, and various sundry other things. Each occurrence gave me a slightly sick feeling that seems synonymous with the word "lost". Sometimes, that feeling grows close to panic.

The good news is that the lost things from my past were found, and "found" is a beautiful word.

In Luke, chapter fifteen, Jesus tells several stories about lost and found.

He tells of the lost sheep and the shepherd's diligent search until he found the errant lamb. He tells of the woman's lost coin and how she searched her whole house to find it (losing something is a great motivation for housecleaning). And He tells of the lost son and the brokenhearted father who waited for his child to come home. In each case, the lost item or person triggered feelings of despair and sorrow. In each case, the finding brought great joy.

When the sheep was found:

> And when he hath found it, he layeth it on his shoulders, rejoicing. And when he cometh home, he calleth together his friends and neighbors, saying unto

them, Rejoice with me; for I have found my sheep which was lost. I say unto you, that likewise joy shall be in heaven over one sinner that repenteth, more than over ninety and nine just persons, which need no repentance (Luke 15:5–7).

When the coin was found:

And when she hath found it, she calleth her friends and her neighbors together, saying, Rejoice with me; for I have found the piece which I had lost. Likewise, I say unto you, there is joy in the presence of the angels of God over one sinner that repenteth (Luke 15:9–10).

When the son came home:

But the father said to his servants, Bring forth the best robe, and put it on him; and put a ring on his hand, and shoes on his feet: And bring hither the fatted calf, and kill it; and let us eat, and be merry: For this my son was dead, and is alive again; he was lost, and is found. And they began to be merry (Luke 15:22–24).

We live in a world of lostness. We have lost our moral compass. We have lost compassion and kindness. We have lost direction and purpose. We have lost our identity in and relationship with God. We have lost hope.

The result is that sick feeling that fills our hearts, the uneasiness that accompanies the news reports, and the outright despair as we face the future.

The funny thing is that our lostness is a choice.

Just like the rebellious son who left his father in the parable that Jesus told, we have chosen our own way over God's way. We have walked away from truth and love and grace and mercy right into the arms of the enemy of our souls, who seeks to kill and destroy.

The good news, the great news, is that the Father calls us and longs for our return. No one has to stay lost. No soul is beyond the Father's care.

Found is a beautiful word, and just as the son returned, any who will repent and turn to the Father today will find His arms open wide. *Dear Father, how stubbornly we have resisted Your love and run from Your care. How many times have we chosen our foolish ways over Your wisdom? Forgive me, Lord. Forgive me. I run to You. Wash me and make me fit for Your kingdom. In Jesus' precious name.*

Think About It:
- Do you identify with the son before or after he returned to the Father?
- Have you experienced the beauty of being found by the Shepherd?
- What does "lost" mean to you?

Rescued

Scarlett—
My sins were like a river.
Flowing—
Dark and swift forever.
Pulling—
Me underneath the water.
Covering the breath of life.

Drowning—
I could swim no longer.
Fading—
As I slipped slowly under.
Struggling—
I wish I could be stronger.
Grasping, I reached for You.

And You pulled me up out of the darkest grave.
You gave Your life, so I could be saved.
You washed me whiter than snow,
So that You love I would know.

Laughing—
Filled with Life's sweetest breath.
Breathing—
Rescued from a certain death.
Living—
Ransomed and set free.
Loving, I reach to You!

For You pulled me up out of the darkest grave.
You gave Your life, so I could be saved.
You washed me whiter than snow,
So that Your love I would know.

Grace in Failure

If we say that we have no sin, we deceive ourselves, and the truth is not in us. If we confess our sins, he is faithful and just to forgive us our sins, and to cleanse us from all unrighteousness.
—1 John 1:8-9

Failure often describes our human state. No one rides at the top of the world forever, and we tend to be our own worst enemies when we attempt to maneuver through the mire of this world dependent upon our own wisdom.

Luke 22 is a chapter of failure.

- Judas failed to remain loyal to Christ, willingly offering to expose Him for money.
- The disciples failed to pray while Jesus bore the sorrow of the coming cross. Instead, He found them asleep.
- Peter failed when he met the challenge of owning his relationship with Jesus. He swore and denied ever knowing Him. He had not taken seriously Jesus' warning about this temptation.
- The leaders failed to believe Jesus' word, even after witnessing the multitude of miracles He had performed.

I can point my finger at Judas and tsk-tsk Peter's disloyalty. I can shake my head at the disciples' failure to pray and wonder how anyone could have failed to believe that Jesus was who he claimed to be. I can, but I won't.

I won't because I, too, have failed. My faith has wavered at times when I couldn't understand how God was working in a situation. My heart has trembled in fear as I faced difficult circumstances. My life has not always been loyal to Christ's teachings, and there have been times that I have failed to regard God's warnings.

I won't because I know how human I am, and God does, too.

The most poignant verse in this chapter to me is verse 61. The rooster has just crowed for the third time. Peter's eyes look up at Jesus, and Jesus is looking at him. Then Peter remembers the word of the Lord, "And the Lord turned, and looked upon Peter. And Peter remembered the word of the Lord, how he had said unto him, Before the cock crow, thou shalt deny me thrice" (Luke 22:61).

While Jesus was on trial for his life, He took time to look at Peter in this moment of defeat. I don't believe His look was one of judgment or anger. I believe His look held love and compassion for Peter and for the frail state of mankind.

I think about Psalm 103 and its description of God's graciousness to us. In verses eleven and twelve, we read, "Like as a father pitieth his children, so the LORD pitieth them that fear him, For he knoweth our frame; he remembereth that we are dust."

The good news, the victory, that I find in Luke, chapter 22, exists in the fact that Jesus did not throw up His hands and refuse to go to the cross when all around Him was nothing but failure. He could have. He could have said, "Father, they are not worth our time. I'm done".

But Jesus didn't. The failures around Him did not move Him from His love or His purpose. In fact, they were the very reason He went on to suffer the despair and agony of the next day.

He bore the cross for our failure.

Failure to be good enough.

Failure to be faithful enough.

Failure to be perfect.

The glorious truth of the gospel is that we could not keep the law, so Christ kept it for us, and then He paid the penalty for all our failures, our sins.

Peter realized that he had failed, and he went out and wept bitterly.

However, later scripture shows us that he didn't stop there. Peter trusted, depended on, the grace that flowed from the cross, and he went on to become a faithful servant of Christ.

Many people surrounded Christ that day. Some continued to mock Him and trust their own rightness. Others ignored the whole situation. But then there were those who saw and, like Peter, came to trust the grace paid for at the cross and so freely given to all who believe.

Today, as failed human beings, we have the same opportunity. We can choose our own way, ignore what Christ has done, or willingly trust Him as we turn to Him for forgiveness and restoration.

I choose Christ.

Father, I have failed so many times. I have failed to love You first in my heart and to love others. I have sought my own way. I have tried to solve problems in my own wisdom and strength, and like Peter, I find myself so broken without You. I am not good enough, faithful enough, or perfect, but You are all these things. I trust You to cleanse me and grow me into what You want me to be. I give myself to You, failure that I am. I love You, Lord.

Think About It:
- What failure are you facing?
- How can you give this failure to God?

Grace When the Storm Comes: Situational Awareness

But the end of all things is at hand: be ye therefore sober, and watch unto prayer.
—1 Peter 4:7

Recently, we had a morning when storms swept through our area before dawn. Phones blared weather alerts, and a glance at the television confirmed a tornado warning nearby. Parked in a state park in our RV, we practiced situational awareness. We monitored the radar, dressed in case a dash was necessary, considered our options for cover, and listened to the blustery wind and rain. The RV shook a little, but thankfully, we were fine.

Situational awareness—being alert to the area and conditions around you, noting danger signs, and staying prepared.

Tornado warnings are not the only reason to practice *situational awareness*.

Jesus told his disciples (and us) to, "Watch therefore: for ye know not what hour your Lord doth come" (Matthew 24:42).

This command followed a discourse on the happenings that will occur before Christ's return. Jesus wanted his followers to be on alert and aware of the troubles that they would face in the world. He wanted us to be prepared for the rising difficulties and dangers.

Jesus talked of wars and rumors of wars, and false saviors. He spoke of conflict, famine, pestilence, and earthquakes. He warned of the persecution of those who follow Him, and He cautioned against the false teachers that would arise (Matthew 24:4–11). He warned that the abundance of sin would cause people's love for God to grow cold (Matthew 24:12). Mark and Luke also record these warnings (Mark

13, Luke 21), and Paul repeated the instruction to watch in 1 Corinthians 16:13 and 1 Thessalonians 5:6.

Watchful anticipation is a theme that runs through the New Testament. It is evident that God intends for us to practice *situational awareness*. How do we do this?

Think about what we did while watching for the tornado.

- **We monitored the situation.** Christians are wise to monitor the occurrences in our world today. While we do not know the day or the hour when our Lord will return, we know He is coming, and He told us to be aware of the things taking place around us. He did not tell us this to make us fearful (more on that in a minute), but to encourage and strengthen us. He is coming back, and we can see His Word taking place today.

- **We made sure we were dressed.** If we are to be ready for the Lord to return, we must be clothed in His righteousness. "I will greatly rejoice in the Lord, my soul shall be joyful in my God; for he hath clothed me with the garments of salvation, he hath covered me with the robe of righteousness, as a bridegroom decketh himself with ornaments, and as a bride adorneth herself with her jewels" (Isaiah 61:10). Christ clothes us in His righteousness when we repent of our sin and call upon Him to save us. Our own righteousness is as "filthy rags," but Jesus died on the cross to provide His righteousness for us. (Philippians 3:9)

- **We considered our options.** Every day we make decisions about what to do and where to go. *Situational awareness* requires recognizing that we have limited time on this Earth. We must pray and ask God to guide us in the best choices for the time we have. "Take ye heed, watch and pray: for ye know not when the time is" (Mark 13:33). "Trust in the Lord with all thine heart; and lean not unto thine own

understanding. In all thy ways acknowledge him, and he shall direct thy paths" (Proverbs 3:5–6). Jesus has called His followers to occupy, stay busy, until He comes (Luke 19:13).
- **We listened to the blustery wind and rain**. We were aware, but we were not afraid. Here, I want to talk about the fact that Jesus did not call us to despair over the world's conditions. In fact, He repeatedly encouraged His followers. Matthew 24:6: "…see that ye be not troubled:" Luke 21:28: "And when these things begin to come to pass, then look up, and lift up your heads; for your redemption draweth nigh." 2 Thessalonians 2:2: "That ye be not soon shaken in mind, or be troubled, neither by spirit, nor by word, nor by letter as from us, as that the day of Christ is at hand."

These are just a few of the encouraging words that Christ left for us. We are to go out into this world as His ambassadors, bearing His name with gladness and joy. We know the end of the story, and that is good news! Storms are sweeping through our world, and it is imperative that Christians practice situational awareness as we serve our Master, Jesus Christ. We are not frightened, but we are aware and prepared to serve Him in and through the difficult days in which we live.

If you do not know Him, then please, and I say this with all the love in my heart, *get dressed* by calling on Jesus and asking Him to save you.

"But what saith it? The word is nigh thee, even in thy mouth, and in thy heart: that is, the word of faith, which we preach; That if thou shalt confess with thy mouth the Lord Jesus, and shalt believe in thine heart that God hath raised him from the dead, thou shalt be saved. For with the heart man believeth unto righteousness; and with the mouth confession is made unto salvation" (Romans 10:8–10).

Father, the storms surrounding me are scary, but I know You are in control. I commit my life and all I love into Your hands. Calm my heart as I serve You. Strengthen my resolve as I seek opportunities to share Your word and Your love. Settle my spirit with Your perfect peace in the midst of the storm. Thank You for being my Shepherd and my King. Dear King of the Universe, I love You.

Think About It:
- What is the greatest storm you are facing at this time?
- Are you dressed for the situation?
- What are your options?
- What verses of scripture support your peace in this situation?

God's Unchanging Grace

Thy faithfulness is unto all generations: thou hast established the earth, and it abideth.
—Psalm 119:90

This morning, I was once again awed by the constancy of God.

I stood at the edge of the Atlantic Ocean and watched as the sun made its entrance—right on time. I watched as its light slowly illuminated the horizon setting the clouds on fire and casting reflections on the calm water, and I saw it suddenly burst into full view as it banished the clouds that had curtained its appearance.

I knew when to be on the beach for the show, because the news reported that sunrise would occur at 7:06 A.M. That is exactly when the sun made its glorious appearance.

Right On Time!

While man can predict the sunrise, he did not create the timing of the daily entrance. God, in the beginning, set in order patterns that shape lives today. We can count on them. We set our watches and turn our calendars. We plan for sleep, work, and play because of God's work in creation.

Tides are determined, and fishermen and ship captains chart their courses. Constellations and planets appear in the night sky. Sunrise and sunset are communicated. Seasons change, and the moon moves through its phases each month.

The laws and patterns of nature, not happenstance but planned, continue day after day, month after month, year after year, with little notice. Things are as we expect them to be, and they are to quote God, "very good" (Genesis 1:31).

Constant. We use many words to describe this attribute of God—faithful, steadfast, unwavering—all of them pointing to His unending care for His creation. The laws He set in place in the beginning ensure that the world keeps turning.

God gave laws to guide our behavior as well, and, as with nature, it is only when we deviate from His way that confusion and disarray occur.

When we violate (disobey or discount) the law of God's supreme sovereignty, we become ruled by the vagaries and capriciousness of man. (Exodus 20:3)

When we violate the law of God's holiness, our world is overcome with irreverence and vulgarity. (Exodus 20:7)

When we violate the law of love, families and lives are destroyed, hearts are broken, children are discarded, and generations are damaged. Relationships fail to thrive, and the very framework of society teeters. (Exodus 20:14)

When we violate the law of truth, deceit and treachery rule the day. Each person does that which is right in their own eyes (Proverbs 12:15). People grasp what is not theirs and are never satisfied. Our work ethic fails as each person seeks to grab what he can. (Exodus 20:15-16)

When we violate the law of life, children grow up without fathers, mothers lose their children, and fear terrorizes the living. The young and the old are discounted and considered expendable for convenience's sake. (Exodus 20:13)

When we violate the law of authority and honor, life is out of whack. Children tell their parents what to do, and society spins on the whims of individual preferences. (Exodus 20:12)

When we violate the law of rest, our lives are distracted and disturbed. We fritter like butterflies with no place for calm. (Exodus 20:8)

God is sovereign, and God is constant. He tells us that He is the same "yesterday, today, and tomorrow" (Hebrews 13:8). When we walk within His law, we find His constant presence and provision. (Exodus 20:6)

Is there grace when we fail? Absolutely! God sent His Son, Jesus the Christ, to pay the penalty for our sins and failures and to offer us a way back to the Father. His forgiveness requires recognition and turning from our sin, which is called repentance. As we turn, we must trust His provision of the Savior. This is faith. Once we turn, we are on a new path that follows His way. This is obedience.

Our world screams like a rebellious child wanting cheese puffs, while the Father offers the abundance of His larder. Until we turn and trust and obey, we will continue to bang our heads against the proverbial wall seeking our own way, which leads to our destruction (Proverbs 16:25).

God has not and will not change! We must turn and trust and obey.

Oh, what blessing comes when we turn and trust and obey!

Father, thank You for being the same yesterday, today, and forever, for holding this world, for holding me. Thank You that I can depend on Your mercy and Your grace today and forever. Thank You for being faithful even when I am not.

Think About It:
- Take a few moments to meditate on the constancy of God.
- What are you most thankful for?
- How do you depend on his unchanging grace?
- How do you depend on God's faithfulness?

Grace for Wise Building

Therefore whosoever heareth these sayings of mine, and doeth them, I will liken him unto a wise man, which built his house upon a rock.
—Matthew 7:24

I remember singing the chorus, "The wise man built his house upon a rock, house upon a rock, house upon a rock."[11] with my Sunday School students. It is based on the account in Matthew 7:24-27 in which Jesus spoke to the multitude about the wise man and the foolish man. One man built his house upon a rock, while the other built his house upon the sand.

This passage occurs at the end of the Sermon on the Mount, and Jesus had presented some hard truths to the people—to us.

Things like:

- The way to eternal life is a narrow way, while the way to destruction is broad.
- Being known by the fruit we bear.
- Getting the log out of your own eye before trying to get a speck out of someone else's.

After all the teaching, Jesus ends with the story about two men.

> Therefore whosoever heareth these sayings of mine, and doeth them, I will liken him unto a wise man, which built his house upon a rock: And the rain descended, and the floods came, and the winds blew, and beat upon that house; and it fell not: for it was founded upon a rock. And every one that heareth these sayings of mine, and doeth them not, shall be likened unto a foolish man, which built his house upon the sand: And the rain descended, and the floods came, and

the winds blew, and beat upon that house; and it fell: and great was the fall of it (Matthew 5:24–27).

Two men who chose to build on two different foundations—rock and sand.

Here is what struck me as I read this story again: life happened to both men.

They both had rain.

They both had floods and wind.

Both houses suffered from the elements' viciousness.

One house stood. One house fell.

The only difference was the foundation.

Rock or sand.

Make no mistake. There is only one foundation that will get you through the storms in this life. There is only one wise way to build your life. Only one foundation is eternal.

The Rock is Jesus. He is the strong foundation. We build on Him when we trust Him for salvation.

Any other foundation or belief system with leave you with a flattened house—an eternity of destruction.

We are facing storms in our world, and everyone will experience the difficulties of life, the heartaches, and the trials. We are not immune.

Do you want to make it through? Do you want your house to stand for eternity?

Turn to Jesus. Trust Him. Obey Him.

There is no other way.

"Jesus saith unto him, I am the way, the truth, and the life: no man cometh unto the Father, but by me" (John 14:6).

Father, You have provided the strong foundation for this life and for eternity. You have given us Jesus. I trust Him to carry me through the storms of this life and safely into life everlasting. Thank You for showing me how to build wisely. Let my spiritual house grow in obedience to You. In Jesus' name I pray.

Think About It:
- What foundation are you building on?
- How confident are you as you face the storms of this life?

Bad News and Then There's Grace

Against Thee, Thee only, have I sinned, and done this evil in Thy sight:
—Psalm 51:4

When we sweep away the world's detritus that clutters our hearts and emotions, we realize that our sin is direct rebellion against God's ownership of our lives. We like to lessen the blackness of our sin by confessing the surface missteps we have made. We call them mistakes or slip-ups. We sound spiritual, but it is an illusion that has failed to touch our hearts.

David, however, went straight to the core of the problem when he prayed, "against Thee, Thee only, have I sinned, and done this evil in Thy sight" (Psalm 51:4). He hadn't *just* wronged Bathsheba through an illicit relationship. He hadn't *just* made a bad military decision that caused Uriah's death. He had broken his relationship with the God of creation. In misusing his power as king, he had placed himself above God's plan for his life. He had ripped the wheel of control out of the Father's hands and promptly driven into the ditch of destruction. He had failed to honor God's Lordship of His life, claiming the throne for himself instead. He had repaid God's love and provision with rebellion and greed.

We may not have committed the same sins as David, but our hearts are no different. We are in rebellion against God's way for our lives. We pray, "God, forgive me for talking about Jane," without acknowledging that we don't love Jane as God commanded. We ask God to forgive our sins, without recognizing that our sins are fueled by the seed of rebellion, which fights against God's loving control of our lives. We are broken, and as with any disease, we must address the cause of this brokenness if we are to be healed.

I know that we are human and that perfection won't happen until Christ returns, but I also know that it doesn't do much good to spray air freshener in a house if meat is left rotting in the kitchen waste basket. The Holy Spirit convicts me to deal with the rottenness of rebellion, to look past the surface symptoms revealed in my actions to the core of my relationship with God.

Jesus forced Simon Peter to do this. It wasn't by accident that He asked Peter three times, "Do you love Me?" (John 21). Jesus knew that Peter's failure on the night before the crucifixion wasn't just a weakness of the flesh; it was a problem of the heart—of Lordship.

Sin is serious, and we must understand that it is a heart condition that is demonstrated in what we do. We can't just stop doing something and think, I'm good now. Like David, we must ask God for a new heart (Psalm 51:10). God works on us from the inside out.

The good news, no, the absolutely breathtaking news, is grace. There is life and purpose after failure, and God wants us, even though we have rebelled against Him, even though we fail over and over again. David sought forgiveness in Psalm 51, but his prayer also included restoration (v. 12) and a plan for service (v. 13-15).

God's word to the hurting and damaged today is "it is not too late." God specializes in rebuilding the broken. God loves you, and He wants you. He will fulfill His plan in your life. He did it for David.

"Create in me a clean heart, O God; and renew a right spirit within me" (Psalm 51:10).

Dear Father, You are the healer and the mender of broken hearts. You gave your only Son to pay the penalty for my sin, so that I could be cleansed from sin's curse. He did not die in vain. I thank You for forgiving me and calling me your own. Thank You for salvation. Thank You for Jesus and the price He paid. Help me to live every day of my life in thanksgiving to You. In Jesus' name I pray.

Think About It:
- Read Psalm 51 and think about the words that David prayed. Are they words that speak to your own heart's needs?
- How can you use David's prayer as a pattern for your own prayer?

Grace for the Broken

When Jesus heard it, he saith unto them, They that are whole have no need of the physician, but they that are sick: I came not to call the righteous, but sinners to repentance.
—Mark 2:17

The early morning beach stretched out before me, littered with the debris of the previous night's tide. Shrimp trawlers dotted the horizon, busy bringing in their catch, and the freshening breeze foretold the cold front moving closer. Calm waves lapped gently, seeming to have forgotten the anger of last week's storm.

Shells were everywhere. Clam shells, moon shells, whelks, tiny periwinkles, oyster shells and abalone joined an array of broken pieces entwined with seaweed and grasses. Shells so numerous that my footsteps crunched even though I tried to be careful. Sand dollars, waiting on the next tide, were spaced out as they covered themselves in the damp sand. I even found one almost perfect angel wing.

I confess that I am slightly obsessive about shells. I have searched for, examined, and collected them since childhood. My footprints on the beach are vaguely reminiscent of the Family Circus cartoons[12] of the past, zigzagging back and forth between water and dune as I spy various interests. Jars of collected shells occupy the shelves in our home, and I find it difficult to part with any of them.

In recent years, diminishing shelf space has forced me to be more selective. Now, while I enjoy them all, I look for the perfect specimens, bypassing the broken, like a treasure hunter in search of gold. I may walk the entire beach and only pick up one or two to carry with me.

Today, as I viewed the beauty under my feet, I thought about that.

I picked up a broken abalone with its shiny rainbow of color. I found a whelk, long discarded by its owner and pitted from its interaction with waves and sand, that had become home to barnacles and other minute sea creatures. And while there were many living sand dollars at the edge of the waves, I particularly noticed the broken ones that had not survived the journey from sea to sand.

Broken. "Broken, but beautiful", I heard God's whisper in my soul.

God loves the broken. He picks up the broken. He redeems the broken, and they become His trophies of grace.

Some days, I tromp through this world of broken people, and I fail to see their beauty or their worth to God. Like the shells, they crunch under my feet, while I go about my business of everyday, choosing whom I will notice.

I was broken, but God reached down and redeemed me.

I was covered in the mud and debris of the world, but He washed me clean through the sacrifice of His Son, Jesus Christ.

I was not and am not perfect, but God treasures me.

My prayer on the beach this morning asked God to open my eyes to the beauty of the broken and to open my heart to treasure the broken, knowing how much He loves them. He picks up the broken that turn to Him and washes them clean. He redeems the broken, and they become trophies of His grace.

I know, because He did it for broken me.

As usual, I brought back a variety of specimens from the beach today, but many were not perfect. A broken sand dollar, part of an abalone, an empty crab shell, and the top of a lovely whelk were part of my bounty. They will join my collection to remind me that

God loves the broken.

God picks up the broken and washes them clean. God redeems the broken, and He calls me to love them, too.

"But God commendeth his love toward us, in that, while we were yet sinners, Christ died for us" (Romans 5:8).

Father, thank You for loving me, a broken soul, for redeeming me and making me whole again. Thank You for seeing beauty where sin had left destruction. Open my eyes and my heart to the broken around me. Give me Your eyes to see their beauty and their need. Open my mouth to tell them of Your love for them. Let my hands and my heart be open for You. In Your precious Son's name, I pray.

Think About It:
- Has God redeemed your brokenness?
- Do you notice the people that you pass each day?
- What are the ways that you can reach out to the broken?

Grace for a Letter from Paul

Finally, brethren, farewell. Be perfect, be of good comfort, be of one mind, live in peace; and the God of love and peace shall be with you.
—2 Corinthians 13:11

In our technologically savvy world of emails, texts, and quick responses, I love letters. Outdated they may be, but as I wade through the advertisements and bills that flood the mailbox, a handwritten missive addressed to me gives pleasure and excitement.

Just last week, I received a letter from one of my granddaughters. She is learning to address envelopes, and she colored a picture and wrote me a note. What a delight.

The Apostle Paul was a letter writer. When a church was established, he used letters to communicate God's teachings to the believers. He wrote from prison, and he wrote while serving churches. Sometimes, the letters were joyful, like the one he wrote to the Philippians. Always Paul's letters included encouragement and instruction. Sometimes, Paul addressed problems in the church to which he was writing. This was the case when he wrote to the church of Corinth.

The Corinthian letters contain some of scripture's most beautiful teachings. Take for instance the description of love in 1 Corinthians 13 or the teaching regarding Christ's resurrection in 1 Corinthians 15. Still, as I read 1st and 2nd Corinthians, I see the struggle Paul had as he addressed sinful lifestyles and unholy attitudes and beliefs that were present in the church.

The Corinthians challenged Paul's apostleship and his ministry, though. They discounted the sacrifices he had made on their behalf, and they followed false teachings. This led to their unholy behavior, which included sins as grievous as incest. The church suffered from divisions and squabbling. The church members, while living in a heathen city, more closely resembled their environment than their identity in Christ. Paul's heart broke as he attempted to bring their hearts back to the God of their salvation.

When I read the last chapter of Second Corinthians, I notice something. Paul's letters often end with greetings and thanksgiving to the various members of the church to whom he was writing. For example, Romans 16 is almost entirely filled with specific acknowledgments and greetings to the people in the church. This is not true in the last chapter of Second Corinthians, however. Instead, Paul ends this book with the admonition for the people to examine their hearts and to do no evil. Then, in verse eleven, he gives four succinct instructions.

Be perfect. In other words, Paul was telling the Corinthians to grow up. It was time to put away the childish and selfish divisions that defined their fellowship. It was time to grow into spiritual maturity and not follow egotistical desires. It was time to leave sinful lifestyles behind. These two words, be perfect, call the believers to work toward maturity of faith and the strengthening of the fellowship. The next three commands give guidance on how to do this.

Be of good comfort. This teaching is saying more than to be satisfied and satiated in self. Instead, as I take comfort in God, I am to be a good comforter to others. I have a responsibility and privilege to look out for my brothers and sisters in Christ. And I am to do this with joy.

Be of one mind. When we have the mind of Christ as the second chapter of Philippians directs us, we can be of one mind with our fellow believers. This instruction moves me past my own way and calls me to consider and support others. It requires that I grow up into Christ's way, and it will result in me comforting and supporting others.

Live in peace. This peace begins first with my relationship with God. If I have peace with God, I can be at peace with others. Paul was not issuing a generic greeting of peace. He was telling the Corinthians to actively seek peace in their relationship with God and to let that peace be evidenced in their relationships with each other.

If we want to live lives pleasing to God, if we want our churches to be lighthouses for others, these instructions are as valuable to us today as they were to the members of the Corinthian church.

It is time for us to grow up, to leave behind the attitudes of selfish ambition and seek God's purpose. It is time for us to seek to comfort rather than to be comforted, to reach out to other believers. It is time for us to submit our minds to the mind of Christ, so that we can live in unity and peace with our fellow believers.

Our churches and our lives, like those of the Corinthians, are often more focused on self than on Christ, more aligned to our personal preferences than His calling. If the Apostle Paul could visit today, I believe his instructions to our churches would still focus on these four principles. We can claim these instructions for our lives today, and we will do well to heed them.

Father, You have not changed Your mind about how we are to treat each other in Your family, nor have You changed how You want us to live. Help me to align myself to Your standards rather than those of the world. Let my life reflect Your grace rather than the latest trends displayed in social media. Let my lips speak Your words in Your love. Grow me in Your knowledge and in Your Spirit, so that I may represent You well in this troubled world.

Think About It:
- Does your church fellowship remind you more of the world or of scripture?
- Are you uplifted by your Christian friends?
- Do you uplift them in the world?
- How could this change?

Grace for the End Times

For God hath not appointed us to wrath, but to obtain salvation by our Lord Jesus Christ, Who died for us, that, whether we wake or sleep, we should live together with him.
—1 Thessalonians 5:9–10

Advertisements abound in magazines, on the internet, and on television. "Make this investment!" "Prepare your portfolio!" "Buy gold." "Diversify." "Protect your riches, your retirement, your way of life!"

I believe in being a wise steward, but the fifth chapter of James begins with a warning to those who put riches first. While being well off is not a sin, making riches a priority over God is. It is clear from the scathing remarks in verses one through six of this chapter that riches will not get me where I want to go.

After that warning, though, James offers some advice to believers (I know the advice is to believers because he called them "brothers"). His advice is for the time before the coming of the Lord, time that scripture tells us will become more and more challenging for believers and for all people. Timely advice for sure.

Be patient. Twice in verses seven and eight, James tells believers to be patient. Be patient as we wait for Christ's return. Do not get caught up in frenzy or fright. Do not give up on God. Wait. God knows what He is doing, and He will be on time.

Establish your heart. Make it firm or determined. Set it in a state of permanence. Set your heart on God and His word, and do not be swayed by the philosophies and arguments of this world.

Grudge not one against another. Time is too short for pettiness and self-centered thinking. Let go of the hard feelings. Forgive.

Endure. Stand fast. Do not give up! We have the examples of God's people in the Bible to encourage us in hard times. There will be suffering and affliction. Think of Joseph and Paul. Remember Jesus! "Behold, we count them happy which endure" (James 5:11).

Swear not. Watch your words. James spent most of chapter three describing and warning about problems with the tongue. Here he makes it short. Don't swear. Let your yes be yes and your no, no. The more we justify or quantify, the more we open ourselves up to wrong speaking.

Pray. If you are sick or afflicted, pray. If you need wisdom, ask. Prayer opens our heart to the Father, and our ears to His heart. Pray, and let your brothers and sisters in Christ pray with you.

Confess. Now is not a time to harbor sin in our hearts. Nor is it time to try to paint a picture of piety. This is the time to be real before God and with our fellow believers.

I do not know when Christ will return, but I know He will. If He tarries until after I am called Home in death, I will still have lived through my last days. No matter what, this is the time to hold closely to Him and to stand for Him.

God help me to stand firmly grounded in Him.

Father, this world is not my home, and sooner or later I will return to You. Whether You return or call me home through death, I will not remain here forever. Let my heart be established and strong as I live here for You. Let my life be transparent as I live for You. Let me patiently serve with compassion and joy each day and let my soul shine for You through the darkness in this world. I stand on Your eternal promises, not the shaky ground of this land. I am secure in who You are. You are my fortress, my Savior, my God. Thank You for keeping me through the muddle around me. Thank You for Your Grace. In Jesus' name I pray.

Think About It:
- How does James' advice for end times help focus you for the week ahead?
- What most concerns you about the end times?
- How can you commit those concerns to God?

Secure

I will not fear the things to come
nor panic at the fray,
for God's sure love remains steadfast
and holds me every day.

No trial or twist can overturn
or tear me from His hand.
No power on Earth can overcome,
for in His strength I stand.

He stills my anxious heart with love
and fills me with His grace.
My victory lies in His love—
a mighty, conquering place.

God's Magnum Opus: His Grace Magnified

Thou art worthy, O Lord, to receive glory and honor and power: for thou hast created all things, and for thy pleasure they are and were created.
—Revelation 4:11

God could have done anything, created anything.

After all, He created the vast expanses of space and spangled it with stars. He created the colors that sparkle on butterflies and bluebirds and that permeate every part of creation. He dreamed up the principles that make our sky appear blue and cause reflections in ponds and rivers and oceans.

He did it all—perfectly.

Then He chose to create man. He didn't just speak man into existence either. He got His hands dirty and molded the first man with exact precision. He breathed His very breath into the man. He gave Him the garden with work to do, the animals and plants. And when the man needed companionship, God formed the woman from the man. It was perfect.

God gave them minds to think.

He gave them hearts to feel and love.

He gave each of them the freedom to choose.

God did it all, and He proclaimed it very good (Genesis 2:31).

God gave mankind the gift of this world and trusted us to honor Him with this gift.

We have failed.

Paul said it well in the first chapter of Romans, "Who changed the truth of God into a lie, and worshipped and served the creature more than the Creator, who is blessed for ever" (Romans 1:25).

Our priorities are all wrong. We arrogantly scream 'science' while ignoring the One who designed every principle of science. We set all our hope in this world, which is temporary at best, while turning away from the One who can keep us eternally.

Mankind has rebelled, chosen his own way, and shaken his proverbial fist at the Father who sought and seeks only to love and redeem us.

Man was God's crowning creation—His magnum opus. God could have done anything, created anything. He chose to create man and woman.

In His desire for man's good, God prepared a way of redemption from our fall, from our sin.

That way is Jesus. Jesus is our way back to a relationship with the Father. He is the only way (John 14:6).

May our hearts turn back to Him.

May our lives honor Him.

May we echo David's cry, "O LORD our Lord, how excellent is THY NAME is all the earth!" (Psalm 8:9).

Father, in Your love and grace, You have prepared a way for us to return to Your heart. We have been so lost, so sinful, so rebellious toward Your love. Thank You for sending Jesus. I'm sorry for the suffering He bore for my sin, but so thankful that He was willing to bear it. I'm sorry the cross was necessary to buy me back, but I'm so glad Jesus was able to pay the price for my redemption. What an amazing God you are. What an amazing Father. What an amazing Savior. I stand redeemed because of Your mercy and grace. Thank you. Thank you!

Think About It:
- What astounds you most about God's plan of redemption?
- What are you most thankful for?

Resources

1. Warren, Rick. *The Purpose Driven Life: What on Earth Am I Here For?* Grand Rapids, MI: Zondervan, 2002.
2. California Milk Processor Board. *Got Milk?* Advertising Campaign. San Rafael, CA, 1993.
3. Balthasar, Hans Urs von. *Prayer.* San Francisco: Ignatius Press, 1986.
4. Bliss, Philip P. "Dare to Be a Daniel." In *The Broadman Hymnal.* Revised edition. Nashville: Broadman Press, 1940.
5. Shakespeare, William. *Romeo and Juliet.* Edited by Barbara A. Mowat and Paul Werstine. New York: Simon & Schuster, 2004.
6. "Passion." *Merriam-Webster Dictionary*, https://www.merriam-webster.com.
7. Henkes, Kevin. *Chrysanthemum.* New York: Greenwillow Books, 1991.
8. Baum, L. Frank. *The Wonderful Wizard of Oz.* Chicago: George M. Hill Company, 1900. Adapted phrase popularized in *The Wizard of Oz.* Directed by Victor Fleming. Metro-Goldwyn-Mayer, 1939.
9. Anonymous. "The Wheelbarrow on the High Wire." Traditional sermon illustration, author unknown.
10. Anonymous. *"Bloom Where You Are Planted."* Common idiomatic expression, widely used in American vernacular, mid–20th century.
11. Omley, Ann. "The Wise Man Built His House Upon the Rock." Originally titled "The Wise and the Foolish Man," 1948. Public domain. Junior Choir sing-along. Inspire4.com.
12. Keane, Bil. *The Family Circus.* Newspaper comic strip. Syndicated by King Features Syndicate, 1960–present.

Wrapped in Grace: 6-Week Study Guide for Reflection, Prayer, and Growth

This study guide is designed to help you slow down, listen closely, and experience God's grace as a living, sustaining presence. Whether you are studying alone or with a group, allow these weeks to become sacred space—where reflection deepens, praise rises, and peace settles in your heart.

You may move through one week at a time or linger longer where God invites you to rest.

How to Use This Study Guide:
- Begin each week with prayer
- Read the assigned Scripture slowly
- Reflect honestly—there are no right or wrong answers
- Journal freely and listen for God's gentle leading
- End with prayer or praise

Week 1: Grace—God's Unmerited Gift

Scripture Focus: Ephesians 2:8–9

Grace is not something we earn or achieve—it is a gift freely given. This week invites you to let go of striving and receive what God already offers.

Reflection Questions:
- How would you describe grace in your own words?
- Where in your life do you feel pressure to "earn" God's approval?

- What would change if you truly believed grace was enough?

Journal Prompt: Write about a time when God met you with grace when you least expected it.

Prayer: *Lord, help me receive Your grace freely and fully.*

Week 2: Grace in Weariness and Waiting

Scripture Focus: Isaiah 40:31; Psalm 27:14

Waiting can feel heavy and discouraging, yet grace sustains us even when answers are delayed.

Reflection Questions:
- What are you currently waiting on God for?
- How does waiting challenge your faith?
- Where have you seen God's strength supporting you during this season?

Journal Prompt: Describe a season of waiting and how God is meeting you there.

Prayer: *God of patience, renew my strength as I wait on You.*

Week 3: Grace That Heals and Forgives

Scripture Focus: Colossians 3:13

Forgiveness is one of the most powerful expressions of grace—and one of the hardest.

Reflection Questions:
- Is there someone you need to forgive—or ask forgiveness from?
- What fears or wounds make forgiveness difficult?
- How does remembering God's grace toward you change your heart?

Journal Prompt: Write a prayer that releases forgiveness in a difficult situation.

Prayer: *Jesus, soften my heart and help me love as You love.*

Week 4: Grace in Praise and God's Presence

Scripture Focus: Psalm 34:1; Hebrews 13:15

Praise shifts our focus from circumstances to God's faithfulness.

Reflection Questions:
- How does praise affect your perspective during hardship?
- What keeps you from praising God in difficult seasons?
- How can praise become part of your daily rhythm?

Practice: Spend five minutes offering spoken or written praise to God.

Prayer: *Father, let praise rise from my heart in every season.*

Week 5: Grace in Life's Messy Places

Scripture Focus: 2 Corinthians 12:9

God's grace meets us most powerfully in our weakness.

Reflection Questions:
- Where do you feel most vulnerable or inadequate right now?
- How might God be revealing His strength through your weakness?
- What would it look like to trust God with this area?

Journal Prompt: Write about a weakness God may be using to grow your faith.

Prayer: *Lord, remind me that Your grace is sufficient for me.*

Week 6: Living Wrapped in Grace Daily

Scripture Focus: Lamentations 3:22–23; Romans 12:1–2

Grace is not only something we receive—it is something we live out daily.

Reflection Questions:
- What does living "wrapped in grace" look like in your everyday life?

- How has your understanding of grace grown during this study?
- What spiritual practices help you remain rooted in God's presence?

Journal Prompt: Describe the kind of life God is inviting you into moving forward.

Prayer: *Lord, help me walk each day renewed, surrendered, and wrapped in Your grace.*

Closing Reflection:

Grace is not only how we are saved—it is how we are sustained. As you finish this study, remember that God's grace is with you in every season, every struggle, and every step forward.

Come rest.

Come reflect.

Come be wrapped in grace.

Wrapped in Grace: Leader's Guide & 6-Week Study

Purpose of This Study:

Wrapped in Grace invites readers to experience God's unmerited favor not only as theology, but as a lived reality. As a leader, your role is not to "teach answers," but to create space—for reflection, honesty, prayer, and encounter.

This guide is meant to be gentle, adaptable, and Spirit-led.

Preparing to Lead:

Before each session:

- Read the assigned section prayerfully
- Reflect on your own experiences with grace
- Ask God how He wants to move in your group
- Remember: vulnerability invites vulnerability

Group Rhythm (Suggested 60–75 minutes):

- Welcome & Opening Prayer (5–10 minutes)
- Scripture Reading (5 minutes)
- Discussion & Reflection (30–40 minutes)
- Quiet Prayer or Journaling (10–15 minutes)
- Closing Prayer or Praise (5 minutes)

Guidelines for Healthy Group Discussion:

- Confidentiality is essential
- Listen without fixing
- Honor different spiritual journeys
- Allow silence—it is often where God speaks
- Encourage participation but never force sharing

6-Week Study Outline:

Week 1: Grace—God's Unmerited Gift
Scripture: Ephesians 2:8 – 9
Theme: Receiving grace without striving
Discussion Starters:
- How do you define grace in your own words?
- Why is it difficult to receive grace freely?

Leader Tip: Emphasize that grace is not earned—it is received.

Week 2: Grace in Weariness and Waiting
Scripture: Isaiah 40:31; Psalm 27:14
Theme: Trusting God's timing
Discussion Starters:
- What does waiting look like in your life right now?
- How has God sustained you during seasons of delay?

Prayer Focus: Surrender impatience and fear.

Week 3: Grace That Heals and Forgives
Scripture: Colossians 3:13
Theme: Letting grace flow through us
Discussion Starters:
- Why is forgiveness often harder than we expect?
- How does remembering God's grace toward us change our posture toward others?

Leader Tip: Remind participants that forgiveness is a process, not a moment.

Week 4: Grace in Praise and God's Presence
Scripture: Psalm 34:1; Hebrews 13:15
Theme: Praise as an act of trust

Discussion Starters:
- How does praise change our perspective?
- What keeps us from praising God in difficult seasons?

Practice: End with spoken or silent praise.

Week 5: Grace in Life's Messy Places

Scripture: 2 Corinthians 12:9

Theme: Strength in weakness

Discussion Starters:
- Where do you feel most inadequate right now?
- How might God be revealing His grace through your weakness?

Leader Tip: Normalize struggle—grace thrives in honesty.

Week 6: Living Wrapped in Grace Daily

Scripture: Lamentations 3:22–23; Romans 12:1–2

Theme: Walking forward renewed

Discussion Starters:
- What does living "wrapped in grace" look like practically?
- How has your understanding of grace changed over these weeks?

Closing Activity: Invite participants to pray over one another.

Final Encouragement for Leaders:

You are not responsible for transformation—only faithfulness. Trust God to meet each participant where they are. Grace does the rest.

Come rest.

Come reflect.

Come be wrapped in grace.

Prayer & Reflection Page

(This page may be repeated or photocopied.)

Today, I bring before God:

_____
_____
_____
_____

Where I need grace right now:

_____
_____
_____
_____

What I sense God inviting me to release:

_____
_____
_____
_____

A prayer from my heart:

_____
_____
_____
_____

Acknowledgements

Nothing worthwhile can be accomplished in isolation, and that is certainly the case when it comes to this book. While it started as just a kernel of a dream in my heart many years ago, it was watered and nourished by the prayers and support of many people.

First of all, I thank God for the privilege of sharing His grace with readers. All that is good comes from Him. Thank you to Dressed in Love Press. Thank you, Katherine, for taking a chance on me and offering me this opportunity to publish. Thank you to Crystal and all the others on the team who supported me along the way with words of advice and encouragement.

I am blessed to walk alongside my Page 23 Word Weavers' writing group each month. Thank you to Terrance, Nancy, Sam, Linda, and again, Katherine for your insightful critiques and the fellowship we have shared around our writing. My writing has grown because of your challenges. You have pushed me to write more and to write better for the glory of God. Thank you.

I would not be here without the love and support of my GraceSpeak blog readers. You were the first ones who said, "You need to write a book." You were the ones who began praying for me. I wish I could list all the names here, but I would leave out someone if I did. I know who you are, and I cherish you. Know that you had a tremendous part in the production of this book. I see each of you as I read through the pages.

And to my family, who put up with me sneaking away to the computer and carrying notepads everywhere we went and taking pictures of every flower we passed, thank you. Thank you for letting me use our experiences as fodder for lessons that God was teaching. You are such good sports, and I love you more than words can ever say.

Beth Mims was born and raised in the Florida panhandle, where the Gulf Coast's white sands give way to the red clay hills of Georgia. A lifelong educator, she has devoted her career to nurturing both minds and hearts, grounded firmly in her faith in Jesus Christ, which she considers the anchor of her life.

Beth writes and speaks about grace, perseverance, and the faithfulness of her Lord and Savior, drawing from a life rich in family, service, and quiet moments with God. Married to her husband for more than forty years, she considers her family her crowning achievement. She is the proud mother of two daughters and Nana to five cherished grandchildren.

When she is not writing, Beth enjoys traveling and fishing with her husband, tending her flowers, and sweet-talking the hummingbirds that frequent her yard. She is an active member of Word Weavers, International, and her work has been published in *A Time of Singing Poetry Journal*, *Cantos: A Literary and Arts Journal*, and ChristianDevotions.us. Learn more or connect with Beth at: www.bethmims.com.

COMING SOON

How Christmas Came: A Child's Story of Jesus' Birth

Long ago, on a quiet night filled with wonder, God gave the world its greatest gift.

How Christmas Came gently invites young readers into the true story of Jesus' birth—told through a child's eyes and filled with awe, simplicity, and hope. From the angel's joyful announcement to the humble manger in Bethlehem, this timeless story unfolds with warmth and clarity, helping children understand why Christmas is more than lights, gifts, and celebration.

Written with tender language and child-friendly storytelling, this book offers families a meaningful way to share the heart of Christmas together. Perfect for bedtime reading, classroom storytelling, or seasonal traditions, *How Christmas Came* reminds readers of every age that love entered the world in the most unexpected way.

A beautiful introduction to the Nativity story—one that will be treasured and reread for years to come.

www.ingramcontent.com/pod-product-compliance
Lightning Source LLC
LaVergne TN
LVHW021047100526
838202LV00079B/4653